P9-CFV-591

# Great Canadians

Great

A
CENTURY
OF
ACHIEVEMENT

# Canadians

SELECTED BY The Rt. Hon. Vincent Massey
George Ferguson
Maurice Lebel
W. Kaye Lamb
Hilda Neatby

ILLUSTRATED BY Franklin Arbuckle

THE
CANADIAN CENTENNIAL
LIBRARY

# Contents



THE CANADIAN CENTENNIAL LIBRARY

WEEKEND MAGAZINE

McCLELLAND AND STEWART LIMITED

Pierre Berton, *Editor-in-Chief*
Frank Newfeld, *Art Director*
Ken Lefolii, *Managing Editor*

THE CANADIAN CENTENNIAL PUBLISHING COMPANY LIMITED
*150 Simcoe Street, Toronto, Canada*

## *Introduction by Pierre Berton*

In October of 1964, five distinguished Canadian scholars met in Toronto to name, for this book, the twenty-five Canadians whose achievements stand out above all others in the century since Confederation. So formidable was the diversity of talents and accomplishments facing the committee that on the first roll-call they were unanimous in only two choices. These were Emily Carr, the west coast artist, and Sir Frederick Banting, the discoverer of insulin.

In the light of subsequent agreement, this initial lack of common ground seems curious. But it developed that some members of the selection committee had decided in advance that the most obvious choices for a book on Canadian achievement – the statesmen of the past century – ought to be excluded simply because they *are* obvious.

*The committee agreed that these statesmen were all great Canadians*

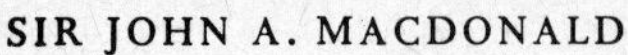

SIR JOHN A. MACDONALD

GEORGE BROWN

SIR WILFRID LAURIER

They had little difficulty in persuading the other members of the committee to this point of view. Every schoolchild, they reasoned, surely understands the achievements of his country's political leaders. If you burden a list like the present one with half a dozen obvious names, then some very important but less well-known figures from the past will unavoidably be neglected. And should there not be a sense of discovery in such a book as this? Why not, then, accept the fact that such giants as Macdonald, Brown, Cartier, Laurier, King and C. D. Howe (all of whom have been treated in another volume in this series) are obviously Canadians of Achievement? Why not set them aside and go on from there?

The committee agreed, then, that statesmen would be outside its terms of reference. This does not mean, however, that there are no politicians in this book. There are four: Bourassa, Chapais, Strathcona and Woodsworth. But none of these men achieved national leadership; and all were chosen for reasons that make their politics incidental to their other achievements.

W. L. MACKENZIE KING SIR GEORGE ETIENNE CARTIER C. D. HOWE

Having agreed upon this somewhat arbitrary rule, the selection committee proceeded further to narrow its terms of reference. It was agreed that, to qualify as Canadians of Achievement during the period of Canada's nationhood, those selected must have made their major contributions after 1867. This ruled out several distinguished Canadians whose important work was done before Confederation.

It was also agreed that promising youngsters did not qualify. The men selected must be of an age to have made their major contribution: after all, one's achievements can scarcely be assessed until one's career has reached or passed its peak. Perhaps for that reason, twenty of the Canadians here enshrined are deceased. Interestingly enough, four of the five living choices are from French Canada.

But, having laid down these rules, the committee still faced a greater question: what, exactly, *is* genuine achievement in a lasting sense? Does it describe a man who achieves something for Canada or something for himself–or both? Is he one who leaves the country to do great things and brings Canada renown simply through his earlier connection with it? Or to qualify must he have lived out his career on Canadian soil? What if his achievement is considerable but of no real benefit to the nation?

On these questions the committee arrived at no hard and fast rules, although its selections indicate its general attitudes.

There was, for example, considerable argument and discussion over the inclusion of Dr. Alexander Graham Bell. Was the Scottish-born Bell, who did so much of his work in the United States, a Canadian? The committee decided that the famous inventor qualified because his telephone research was carried out in Brantford, and so much of his aerial experimentation in Halifax and Baddeck, N.S. Similar discussion arose over the name of Sir William Osler, but here the decision was less difficult. Osler was, after all, Canadian-born, and his influence on the McGill medical school is undeniable.

There was considerable argument over two controversial figures from Canada's past, both of them men of stature in the history books. The name of Louis Riel was hotly debated before it was dropped. "It worries me that he's not on this list," Mr. Ferguson admitted, and Miss Neatby also felt that he should be included "because his political impact was so strong." In the end she agreed with the majority of the committee–especially Mr. Massey and M. Lebel –that his achievement was "not a positive one."

For the same reason, that eloquent French-Canadian nationalist, the historian Canon Groulx, does not appear in this book. "If you want a Quebec historian of stature–and one who influenced his people, then you must pick Chapais," M. Lebel advised. A fellow-historian, Hilda Neatby, agreed; and so, after some discussion, did the rest of the committee.

The committee had little hesitation in choosing another controversial Canadian from the past, Donald Smith, later Lord Strathcona and Mount Royal, whose achievements were often viewed with mixed feelings by his contemporaries and his various biographers. "A remarkable fellow in many ways; a dreadful fellow in many ways," was the way Mr. Massey summed up Strathcona. But he voted for him.

The committee agreed at the outset that all the Canadians it named would be selected for their accomplishments alone, and not because they represented any particular field of endeavour or gender or geographical area. Indeed, it is possible that this is the first list of Canadians ever chosen with no geographical compromises in mind.

For the record it ought to be pointed out that seven of the nominees are French Canadians; that only two are westerners (Emily Carr and "Punch" Dickins); and that only Dr. Bell, Principal Grant (a native of Nova Scotia) and E. J. Pratt have any firm connection with the Atlantic provinces. The majority come from central Canada.

It may also be significant that Miss Carr and Miss Roy stand out as the only women in the group of twenty-five—a revelation that did not at all surprise or disturb Miss Neatby. She said flatly that women, generally speaking, were not people of achievement in the sense that men were—especially men of the century under consideration.

It was another Canadian of achievement, Dr. Brock Chisholm, who once pointed out, rather acerbly, that most history-book heroes turn out to be military men. Is it significant, I wonder, that there is only one soldier in the present selection? And Sir Arthur Currie was chosen less for his military exploits than for his nationalism—it was Currie who preserved the Canadian Corps as a separate military force in World War I. Thus did Currie, in Mr. Ferguson's words, place himself in the foreground of a group of young nationalists "who wanted to create something different in Canada."

In this diverse group there are, it turns out, as many men of reflection as there are men of action. Ten come from the sedentary arts and sciences. Three of these are historians (a fact that may betray the personal bent of some committee members), two are poets, two are painters, two are writers, one is a man of the theatre. Significantly, there are no musicians (except the hopeful amateur, Charles Saunders), and no architects.

There are also, as is proper in a young country, three explorers—one a seaman, one a landsman and the third, of course, an airman. The selection leans heavily towards men of science: there are half a dozen from fields as varied as medicine, engineering and agronomy. But there are only three who could properly be termed captains of industry (Van Horne, Strathcona and Timothy Eaton). There are no sports figures at all, an omission which will no doubt disturb certain sections of a hockey- and football-oriented nation. But the committee was adamant on the subject of athletic heroes who, it believes, are ephemeral figures. It was generally agreed that "they make no impact on future generations."

But then everybody who reads this book is going to quarrel with some of the choices, as indeed the present editor does. For there are, happily, scores of Canadians of achievement and no single list could hope to satisfy all sections of a nation as diverse as this one. (It was a minor miracle that the selection committee was able to complete its task amicably within three hours.)

I would be less than human if I did not feel keenly the omission of certain figures of stature from this book. Had I been a voting member of the committee I should certainly have made a strong case for Dr. Norman Bethune, the first medical man in history to perform blood transfusions in the field and the only Canadian of any achievement known to the six hundred million people of China. I should probably also have reflected my personal bent by pressing for the inclusion of John W. Dafoe, the great prairie journalist. I might also have argued with considerable vigour for men of the calibre of Yousuf Karsh, Sir Adam Beck, Robert Flaherty, Louis Riel, Vilhjalmur Stefansson and Robert W. Service, all of whom have left their considerable mark upon this nation and upon the world.

Yet I cannot quarrel with the present list since it was the product of reasonable and intelligent thought by highly qualified Canadians who know the story of their country as well as any among us. It is to help others know this story a little better, as we approach our hundredth milestone, that this volume was conceived. If some of the names and faces in the pages that follow are strangers to you, I hope they will soon become old friends.

*The editor wanted these men included but the committee overruled him*

CANON LIONEL GROULX
*Quebec historian*

JOHN W. DAFOE
*Prairie editor*

NORMAN BETHUNE
*Revolutionary physician*

YOUSUF KARSH
*Portrait photographer*

SIR ADAM BECK
*Ontario Hydro pioneer*

ROBERT FLAHERTY
*Documentary film maker*

ROBERT W. SERVICE
*Yukon poet*

LOUIS RIEL
*Rebel*

VILHJALMUR STEFANSSON
*Arctic explorer*

# THE SELECTION COMMITTEE

The Right Honourable Vincent Massey, C H

Chairman

Mr. Massey's long and distinguished career in the public service of his country reached its climax in 1952 when he was appointed our first native-born governor-general, a post he held until 1959. He has variously been lecturer in modern history, amateur actor, president of Massey-Harris Ltd., federal cabinet minister, Canadian Minister to the United States, and Canadian High Commissioner in the United Kingdom–among other things. He is the author of several books, not the least of which is the famous "Massey Report" of the proceedings of the Royal Commission on National Development in the Arts, Letters and Sciences. His many awards include the Companion of Honour, the Canada Council Medal and the Albert Medal of the Royal Society. The four distinguished Canadians who sat on this selection committee were chosen at Mr. Massey's suggestion.

Mr. George V. Ferguson

EDITOR-IN-CHIEF
THE MONTREAL *STAR*

Born in Scotland, Mr. Ferguson came to Canada at the age of six and spent his early years in British Columbia and Alberta. His education at the University of Alberta was interrupted by war service. In 1921 he went to Oxford as a Rhodes Scholar and after graduation worked on *The Times* of London. He joined the Winnipeg *Free Press* in 1925, rising to the position of executive editor, a post he resigned in 1946 to join the Montreal *Star*. Well known for his articles on foreign affairs and for his CBC commentaries, he is the author of two books and many thousands of newspaper editorials.

## Dr. W. Kaye Lamb

DOMINION ARCHIVIST
AND NATIONAL LIBRARIAN

Born in New Westminster, B. C., Dr. Lamb was educated at the universities of B.C., Paris and London. He has been an archivist and librarian most of his working life, first for the province of British Columbia (1934-1940), then for the University of British Columbia (1940-1948) and now for the federal government. He is well known for his historical research into the fur-trading era, and was for twelve years president of the Champlain Society. In 1965 he was named president of the Royal Society.

Dr. Maurice Lebel

PROFESSOR OF GREEK, LAVAL UNIVERSITY

Born at St. Lin, near Montreal, Dr. Lebel holds degrees from Montreal, Laval, the Sorbonne, London and Athens in addition to several honorary degrees. Formerly dean of the faculty of the humanities at Laval, he is also a past president of the Royal Society of Canada, of the Canadian Humanities Research Council and of the Canadian Classical Association. A multiple prize-winner in his field, he has published thirteen books, eighteen pamphlets and numerous articles in the learned journals.

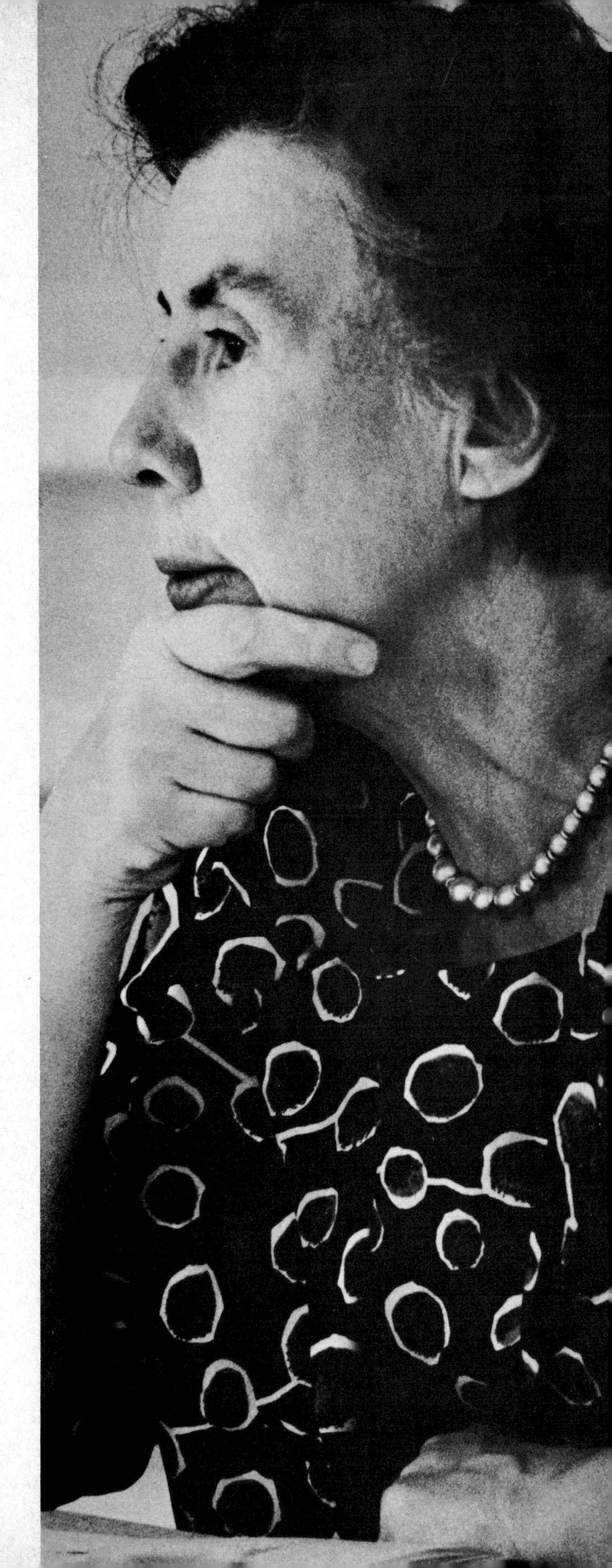

Dr. Hilda Neatby

HEAD OF THE DEPARTMENT OF HISTORY, UNIVERSITY OF SASKATCHEWAN

Born in Sutton, England, and educated at the University of Saskatchewan, the Sorbonne and the University of Minnesota, Miss Neatby has been on the faculty of the University of Saskatchewan since 1936. A member of the Royal Commission on National Development in the Arts, Letters and Sciences, she gained national attention in 1953 with the publication of her contentious indictment of Canadian education, *So Little for the Mind*. A former editor of *Saskatchewan History*, she has published two other books and many articles on education and historical subjects.

# Great Canadians

# Sir Frederick Banting

1891-1941

His discovery of insulin as a remedy for diabetes is considered one of this century's greatest medical advances. Born in Alliston, Ontario, and educated at the University of Toronto, he had just finished war service and was starting practice in London, Ontario, when he conceived the original idea. He took it to Professor J. J. R. Macleod, head of the department of physiology at Toronto's faculty of medicine. Here he and his associates succeeded in isolating insulin. The Nobel Prize followed and a host of other gold medals, prizes, awards and honorary degrees including a knighthood. In 1923 he was appointed professor of medical research at the university, a post he held until he re-enlisted in the Medical Corps in World War II. He was killed in a plane crash in eastern Newfoundland.

10 AM
92- Blood sugar .22
wt.- 11.1.K. dog feeling good
runs around room! frisky.
409- Blood sugar .37.
has not eaten meat, can barely
stand, drinks a great deal!
wt.- 5.9.K.

It was decided to find out
if overdose of the extract
would reduce the blood
sugar in dog 92 below .09 normal.
accordingly at 11.10 AM.
blood was withdrawn (blood
sugar of this sample = .22)
and 20 cc of the extract was
given intravenously. At 11.40 AM
blood withdrawn (blood sugar
and 10 cc extract given. At
12.20 P.M. blood sugar: .06
At 1.00 P.M. Blood
- 30 P.M. Blood
Blood became
stirring with distilled

# *The Catalyst*

*by* LEONARD BERTIN

No Canadian scientist has come near to achieving the public recognition–and gratitude–accorded both at home and abroad to Frederick Grant Banting for his discovery of insulin. The reason is simple. No single scientific discovery has so suddenly changed the fate of so many people.

In North America alone, in 1921, there were more than a million people stricken by diabetes, the condition that a Greek physician two thousand years earlier had cannily described as "the disease in which the flesh melts and is siphoned away in the urine." Countless others in all parts of the world had felt death tap them on the shoulder and experienced the ravenous hunger and unquenchable thirst of "the wasting sickness." Yet no one knew the cause or the cure. In the days before Banting's great discovery there was nothing that anyone could do to stave off the end but restrict diet to a starvation level and wait, as the body grew weaker, infections flourished, eyes were dimmed by cataracts or internal bleeding and fingers and toes became gangrenous.

The wonderful and undeniable fact was that this twenty-nine-year-old Ontario farmer's son, whose postwar surgery in London, Ontario, rarely attracted a single patient, had come to Toronto with an idea and had challenged the giants. With the help of a young student, Charles H. Best, he succeeded where experienced men had tried repeatedly and failed.

Banting, like so many other great men, was not brilliant in his studies but he was dogged and he had an image to live for. He used to speak of the day when, on his way to school, he had seen two builders badly injured in the collapse of a scaffolding. A crowd gathered, and when the doctor arrived his presence was a relief to everyone, Banting later recalled. "I watched every movement of his skilful hands, and in those tense minutes I thought, 'The greatest service to man is in the medical profession.' From that day on it was my greatest ambition to be a doctor."

He graduated from the University of Toronto in the class of 1917. Straightway he joined the Medical Corps and went to France, where he won the Military Cross for tending the wounded under fire while badly wounded himself. Banting must have felt very much wanted by his comrades in the trenches. When war threatened a second time in 1939 Banting, by now almost forty-eight and one of the world's most respected scientific leaders, rejoined the army as a major in an ambulance unit, nine days before war was declared.

Honours had been heaped on Banting, and he was always quick to share them. One reporter wrote: "The discoverer of insulin almost gives the impression that a number of people were working on the problem and he happened to be around when the results were announced." He was equally free with money, and assigned all financial interest in insulin to the University of Toronto. On learning that the House of Commons had voted him an annuity of seven thousand dollars a year for life, Banting–who had once sold his furniture, his car and even his instruments to finance his great experiment–wrote to Best:

> *I have just had a marconigram telling me about the Dominion Government. I wish they would give you an equal amount. Surely blessings are falling on us fast enough now. We must keep our heads.*

But Banting was also jealous of fame. Friends say that when he was told he was to receive the Nobel Prize his first impulse was to refuse it, because it was to be shared with Professor J. J. R. Macleod, the titular but absentee head of his department at the time of the discovery. To a medical gathering he was unable to attend, he sent a telegram that read:

> AT ANY MEETING OR DINNER PLEASE READ THE FOLLOWING MESSAGE: I ASCRIBE TO BEST EQUAL SHARE IN THE DISCOVERY. HURT THAT HE IS NOT ACKNOWLEDGED BY NOBEL TRUSTEES. WILL SHARE WITH HIM. BANTING.

Macleod, following Banting's example, shared his half of the forty-thousand-dollar prize with Dr. J. B. Collip, who had helped to prepare purer forms of insulin but with whom Banting was not on good terms.

Banting's life ended abruptly in February, 1941, when the bomber that was carrying him on a liaison mission to England crashed on a frozen lake in Newfoundland. The obsession to serve was with him until the end. Captain J. C. Mackey, the pilot and only survivor, said later that during the days they waited in deep snow for rescue planes to find them, Banting, desperately injured and delirious, continued to dictate rapidly a long succession of letters, memoranda and statements in technical language that he, Mackey, could not understand.

Banting's lung had been punctured; he was dead long before help came and, as the news flashed around the world, friend and foe joined to honour his memory.

In the twenty years between the discovery of insulin and his death, he had turned his hand to many problems. In all his work, however, he described himself as a catalyst–an agent that promotes a reaction without taking any true part in it. There is no doubt he was handicapped in that he lacked a normal apprenticeship in research. Sir Henry Dale, one of Britain's leading scientists, said of him: "The best reward, from his point of view, would probably have been an opportunity to make good such defects of equipment by some years of quiet and disciplined study."

Banting has been likened to a boy who goes fishing along a famous salmon stream, armed with a bent pin and worm. He caught an enormous fish at the outset and could hardly expect to catch another like it. He contrived in later years to surround himself with a talented group of highly trained young researchers who complemented his own more direct approach. It is interesting, though fruitless, now, to wonder what more he might have achieved, had he started with better equipment.

# Alexander Graham Bell

1847-1922

He invented more than the telephone. He also invented the phototone, paving the way for the film soundtrack and the electric eye, and improved the phonograph record. At Baddeck, N.S., he made some of the first experiments with heavier-than-air craft and later with hydrofoil water craft. Scottish-born, he came to Ontario in 1870 and settled in Brantford and later in Boston, where his work in teaching deaf students (he married one) led to the device that made him famous. Later, he moved to Washington, but he made his summer home at Baddeck where he died. Among his many awards was the *Prix Volta* of France. He used the fifty thousand francs prize money to establish the Volta Laboratory Association.

# *The Sentimental Inventor*

by ROBERT THOMAS ALLEN

One day when I was doing some research on Alexander Graham Bell, the inventor of the telephone, I thought I would phone the historian at the old Bell Homestead, in Brantford, Ontario, for some information. I asked the long-distance operator to get the number for me, and was told I could reach it direct by dialling 112, then 519, then 756-6220. When I had done this, a recorded voice said that I had dialled wrongly and would I please repeat my call. I dialled 112-519-756-6220 again. Finally, miraculously, across sixty miles of forest, farm and river, the telephone rang; but nothing else happened, and I had the eerie feeling that Bell was really there but refused to answer the phone, a device he regarded as one of the rudest instruments ever thought up by man. Nobody but a telephone caller, he sometimes said, would interrupt you while you were having dinner, or sleeping, or taking a bath.

I could imagine him, having come back in spirit, brooding over the things that had happened since the days in the 1870s when he worked like a dog in Boston making a meagre living teaching the deaf to speak and, in his spare time, working on this gadget that let you hear what someone at the other end of the wire was saying. A Japanese could even understand what another Japanese was saying, early marvellers said. Bell could never have figured that today, nearly a hundred years later, few people are able to make out what a teenager, for instance, is saying when she curls over a coloured telephone shrieking, "Oh, no! Oh, NO!" as if someone at the other end were having her limbs lopped off. Bell couldn't have foreseen, either, that wives of out-of-town husbands can hear people who aren't even on the phone ("Is that a woman laughing, George?"). Nor could he have conceived of some telephone addicts, like one woman who calls me every week, sitting, I am convinced, amid cobwebs in some attic, to say that she's calling members of royalty and very important people to tell us about the new sixteen-volume set of Polarized Knowledge published by the Canadian Ultimate Encyclopedia Company, and may one of her vice-presidents call on me?

I felt, somehow, though, that if Bell *had* answered the phone, I would have found him typical of hundreds of thousands of people who have left Canada to make a living in the United States; if I had asked him why he was in Brantford after he had taken out American citizenship papers, he would have bent my ear about Ontario apples,

Canadian cheese, Muskoka sunsets, the Pre-Cambrian shield, the wholesomeness of Canadian people, and the superior way they made tea. In a sense Bell never left Canada. He went to Boston eight months after his Scottish parents brought him to Brantford from Edinburgh for his health, but he came back to Canada every chance he got. Nothing ever weakened his ties with Canada, including his one attempt to get Canadian backing for his experiments. This was when he approached the Honourable George Brown, one of the Fathers of Confederation, who agreed to stake Bell to twenty-five dollars a month for six months in return for half interest in all British and foreign rights in the telephone. He took Bell's specifications for the telephone to England, but apparently was convinced the thing wouldn't work, for he left the specifications in his trunk. He wasted so much time that Bell came dangerously close to losing all American rights in the invention, and he made Bell only one payment of twenty-five dollars.

Bell's loyalty to Canada was the very best lasting kind. It was purely sentimental. As if to renew his contact with basic values, he proudly brought his bride to Brantford, where his mother, following an old-country superstition, broke an oatcake over her head, a custom that must have left this girl from Cambridge, Massachusetts, fascinated by her good neighbours to the north. Although Bell made his first phone call in Boston, got his backing from Americans, and filed his patent in Washington, he often assured the Canadian people that he *thought* of the idea for the telephone in Canada, right on the banks of the Grand River in Brantford. He put Canada in the picture, as we might say today, by stringing some stovepipe wire around a rail fence one time when he was home on holidays, and making the world's first long-distance call–from Brantford to Paris, Ontario.

Bell was proud of his U.S. citizenship, but like many Canadians who have taken out U.S. papers since, he felt that it didn't interfere with his being a Canadian. In later years he established a huge home and laboratory on Cape Breton Island. He paddled around in a canoe, wearing a tam and Scotch tweeds. He had a Canadian and an American flag flying over his property, and when a neighbour complained about the Stars and Stripes he told her that if it bothered her that much he would take down the American flag and leave the Canadian flag flying. By now the invention of the telephone was far behind him, but probably not far enough for Bell. Everybody and his brother had claimed to be the real inventor, and Bell had spent years involved in litigation, digging up documents and scraps of paper to prove that the invention was really his. He was upheld in every court decision, but by now, when he experimented with a new idea in Cape Breton or anywhere else, he labelled everything and recorded it, and made photographs of it and would never throw out a piece of paper with writing on it. He refused to autograph anything, and was cagey about signing letters unless the "sincerely" was right up tight against the body of the letter so that nobody could squeeze another sentence in after he signed it.

Now he was on to something else–something really big–a flying machine. He had a couple of young engineers from the University of Toronto working with him: J. A. D. McCurdy (later lieutenant-governor of Nova Scotia) and F. W. Baldwin, the grandson of the premier of Upper Canada. A flying machine had already been made to work by the Wright Brothers in the States, although few people besides Bell believed this. Bell's group, including a lieutenant in the U.S. Army, Thomas E. Selfridge, and a young motorcycle builder named Glenn Curtiss, had made some tests with a plane of their own. The governor-general of Canada, Earl Grey, watched it fly and said, "Extraordinary! How like a bird!"–but the Canadian government did nothing about helping.

Perhaps my attempted phone call to Bell's original Canadian home had put me in tune with those later days on Cape Breton Island in the early 1900s, but I felt that I could hear Bell say: "You'll probably get this all wrong, being a writer, but you can quote me as saying that someday people will travel by air right here in Canada. I'll tell you more about it later." I picture him starting off for his laboratory, then turning and adding, "But don't call me, I'll call you."

# Joseph Elzéar Bernier

1852-1934

He was Canada's greatest sea explorer. He made twelve voyages of exploration to the arctic, awakening both government and public to its importance and, by establishing police posts on the arctic islands, securing the area for Canada. Before his arctic period he had sailed wooden ships across the Atlantic for sale in Great Britain, and served variously as dockmaster at Lévis, Quebec, manager of an ice company in Montreal (the first in that city) and warden of Quebec's city jail. For his work of exploration he was awarded the Royal Geographical Society's Back Grant. He was the author of four reports on his explorations and a posthumous autobiography.

# *The Master Mariner*

On December 26, 1934, Captain Joseph Elzéar Bernier lay in his bed at Lévis, facing Quebec City. The old salt whose voice had thundered above the tempest's roar . . . the legendary hero who had claimed the entire arctic archipelago of North America for Canada . . . the Ulysses of unlimited energy who never made a decision without consulting his gentle wife . . . the adventurer who had survived so many shipwrecks – Bernier was now meeting his death at the end of his eighty-third year.

He seems in retrospect to have stepped directly from a Conrad sea story. In his long career he had crossed the Atlantic 269 times. He had commanded 105 ships. He had been emulated by the greatest polar explorers of his day – Nansen, Amundsen, Scott, Shackleton, Peary, Byrd – all of whom were his friends. He was truly a "master mariner and arctic explorer," the phrase used to describe him in his posthumous *Narrative of Sixty Years at Sea.*

He had been raised in the great days of sail and both his father and grandfather before him had been shipmasters. Born at L'Islet beside the St. Lawrence River on New Year's Day, 1852, he had embarked for the Mediterranean at the age of three – in time to watch and remember the sacking of Sevastapol during the Crimean War. He was a ship's boy at twelve and master of a brigantine at seventeen – "the youngest skipper in the world," as he later wrote.

It was while ploughing the Atlantic, on several of the twenty-two record crossings that won for him the famous Blue Ribbon, that Bernier began to dream of sailing into the far north. Oddly enough he completed his study of the arctic not on shipboard but in prison in Quebec City. He was governor, not inmate, a post offered him in 1895 – and a strangely sedentary job for a man who had

*by* ROGER LEMELIN

known the untamed freedom of the seas. Still, it furnished him the leisure to prepare thoroughly for future adventure. He quit in 1897 and after much badgering of the federal government succeeded in mounting his first trip north during the winter of 1904-05 on his famous three-masted steamer *Arctic*.

But his most important voyage took place three years later, in July of 1908. The Prince of Wales himself (soon to be George V of England) was on hand at Dufferin Terrace to wish the *Arctic* godspeed. Fifteen warships fired salvos. Bands played *Rule Britannia* and *The King* on shipboard and from the cliffs above. And Bernier set off for the unknown; his orders: to sail as far north as possible.

The following April he could write with a pride that manages to show through the opening lines of his official report: "I have the honour to submit my report of the voyage of the Dominion Government steamer *Arctic* to the northern waters contiguous to that part of the Dominion of Canada already annexed and for the further purpose of annexing British possessions as far west as longitude 141 degrees."

From the 60th degree of longitude to the 141st, from the tip of the continent to the 90th degree north, Bernier had claimed the arctic for Canada.

In July, 1910, Bernier sailed again for the arctic, this time in an attempt to repeat Amundsen's feat of sailing through the Northwest Passage. He dreamed of leaving Quebec City, navigating the icy straits of the Arctic Ocean, and arriving at Vancouver. It has been said that tears welled in his eyes when, off Melville Island and far short of his goal, he realized that too many ice floes barred his path to make victory possible.

The first war interrupted his arctic explorations but added, uncomfortably, to his experience. In the midst of a storm, near the coast of Ireland, his ship sank from under him. Fortunately he was travelling in convoy and the crew was saved. True to tradition Bernier was the last to be taken off; the water was lapping the decks before he left.

In England, at a reception, he found himself suddenly embraced by a woman unknown to him who finally identified herself as a grateful relative of Sir John Franklin, the explorer who had vanished forever in the arctic in 1847 and whose memory Bernier had honoured. He was later to say with gallantry and dry humour that his "adventure in the Atlantic and the reception by the impulsive lady, I have always regarded as my two most exciting adventures, one at sea, the other on land."

In 1927, at the Canadian government's request, Bernier set off for Hudson Bay. He was seventy-five years old but his task was vitally important: it was his job to study the possibility of a new export route to Europe for prairie grain funneled through the subarctic port of Churchill. As a result the prairies now ship twenty million bushels a year by this route. Two years later Bernier made his last arctic voyage—again to Hudson Bay. Then, after hundreds of thousands of miles of ocean navigation, he quit the sea forever.

He spent five peaceful years at Lévis, fishing and occasionally travelling. The Pope made him a Knight of the Equestrian Order of the Holy Sepulchre and on great occasions he could often be seen, standing proudly at attention in his bright uniform, beside Cardinal Villeneuve and other ecclesiastical figures. In 1934 the great explorer assisted at the mass celebrating the quatercentenary of the discovery of Canada by Jacques Cartier. It was fitting; the two names of Bernier and Cartier could almost merge in a single glory.

He died the following December, a simple, sincere Christian, after a few days of illness and happily without anguish, one hand clasped in that of his wife. He had remained steadfast to the end, keeping a promise made years before to Sir Wilfrid Laurier, who had worried about the dangers Bernier was then encountering.

"As my father and his father before him," the captain told the prime minister, "I shall die in bed." And so he did, with his eyes fixed on the image of the Madonna, who for him had always been The Star of the Sea.

# Henri Bourassa

PREMIERE ANNEE—No. 1 MONTREAL, LUNDI, 10 JANVIER 1910 UN SOU LE NUMERO

ABONNEMENTS :

Edition Quotidienne :

Edition Hebdomadaire :

# LE DEVOIR

Rédaction et Administration :
71A RUE SAINT-JACQUES, MONTREAL.

TELEPHONE :
REDACTION : Main 7460.
ADMINISTRATION : Main 7461

Directeur : HENRI BOURASSA.

FAIS CE QUE DOIS !

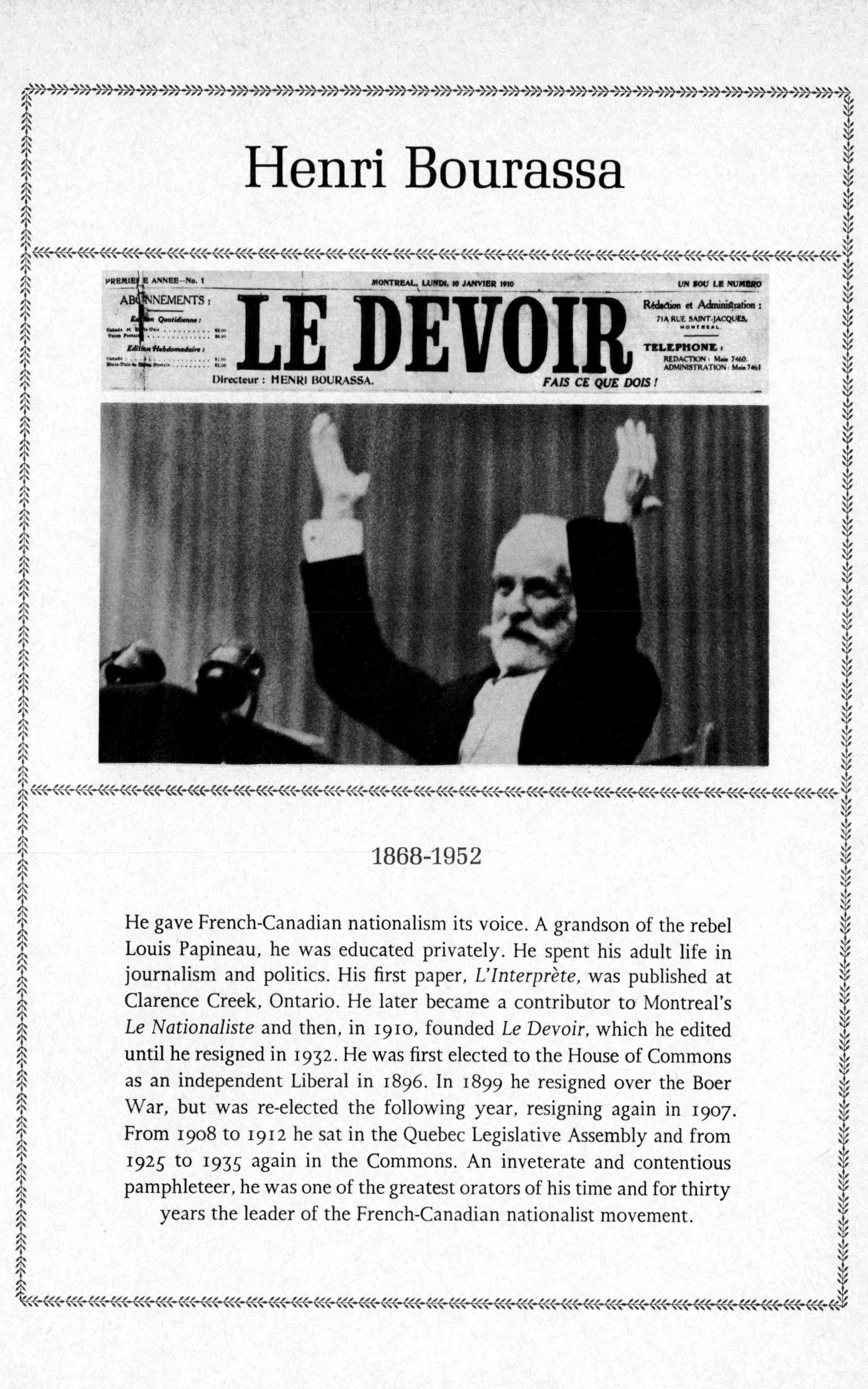

1868-1952

He gave French-Canadian nationalism its voice. A grandson of the rebel Louis Papineau, he was educated privately. He spent his adult life in journalism and politics. His first paper, *L'Interprète*, was published at Clarence Creek, Ontario. He later became a contributor to Montreal's *Le Nationaliste* and then, in 1910, founded *Le Devoir*, which he edited until he resigned in 1932. He was first elected to the House of Commons as an independent Liberal in 1896. In 1899 he resigned over the Boer War, but was re-elected the following year, resigning again in 1907. From 1908 to 1912 he sat in the Quebec Legislative Assembly and from 1925 to 1935 again in the Commons. An inveterate and contentious pamphleteer, he was one of the greatest orators of his time and for thirty years the leader of the French-Canadian nationalist movement.

# *The Unheeded Prophet*

*by* CLAUDE RYAN

Of all the French Canadians who have left their mark on Canadian politics, none except perhaps Wilfrid Laurier and Maurice Duplessis has enjoyed a deeper and more lasting influence than Henri Bourassa.

The founder of *Le Devoir* never headed a government. He was not even a cabinet minister. Power eluded him all his life. But influence he had to an extent that often made some of his arch-enemies, like the great John W. Dafoe of the Winnipeg *Free Press*, claim that he was the real inspiration behind Laurier. "I know," Dafoe once wrote to a French-Canadian friend, "that you boast that you have beaten Bourassa and put him out of business; but as a matter of fact he has conquered you. He may not command your allegiance but he controls your minds. You all think his thoughts, talk his language, echo his threats . . ."

Bourassa's career was a mixture of success and failure. At certain times he seemed to hold the future of French Canada in his hands. At other times he was more or less forgotten.

In 1896, at twenty-seven, Bourassa was elected MP for the rural constituency of Labelle, under Laurier's banner. But even then he was a peculiar type of party man. He insisted that he not receive one penny from the party chest and that he conduct his campaign himself. He was determined to preserve his personal independence.

The Boer War soon provided him with one of the leading themes of his career. Pressed by English-Canadian opinion, Laurier had to opt for active Canadian participation in the war. Bourassa claimed that the decision had been inspired from London. He criticised Laurier for bypassing parliament. This split marked the beginning of a sixty-year crusade in favour of a more indigenous brand of Canadian nationalism. What he opposed was not Canada's participation in the defence of civilization but an immoderate inclination on the part of most Canadian politicians to take sides with Great Britain without first considering world problems in a strictly Canadian perspective.

On the domestic front Bourassa felt from the outset that French Canadians were becoming the losing partners in Confederation. This soon led him to a break with Laurier. Laurier was a man of government; he had deep principles but he had the conviction that those principles could not be fully applied overnight. Bourassa was a man of ideas; to him, a principle that went unapplied was being violated.

Because of his firm attitude Bourassa was feared but never really accepted by English Canada. French Canadians looked on him as their most authentic champion, but at the same time they kept their allegiance to Laurier and Lapointe. Bourassa, it seems, was regarded by them as the most articulate exponent of their deep political aspirations, but for the realization of their dreams they preferred to give their votes to practical men whom they trusted as long as they were continually challenged by a man like Bourassa.

As a maternal grandson of the rebel leader Louis-

Joseph Papineau, Bourassa seemed destined to play a revolutionary role in the emancipation of French Canadians. But he was also, through his father, the inheritor of a strongly conservative tradition. All his life he seemed to wrestle with himself. As long as he had a clear-cut fight to wage against Laurier's excessive flexibility toward English Canada, the basic contradiction in Bourassa's personality went unnoticed. But after World War I, it became obvious that Bourassa would soon be reduced to a minor role. During his long feud with Laurier, Bourassa had defended the rights of French Canadians because he felt that the moral compact of 1867 had been broken. He believed that a political society based on the equality of two different peoples was not only feasible, but noble in itself and highly desirable. He dreamed of a Canada that would accommodate in its bosom two nations as different as the French and the English.

But he had never been an unqualified advocate of the glorification of the French-Canadian nation as such. The new Quebec nationalism of the 1920s sought to achieve for French Canada a much larger measure of collective autonomy than Bourassa had ever thought of. The new nationalists were naturally led to seek a political instrument for the realization of their objective, and found it in the so-called "National State of Quebec."

Bourassa saw in the new ideas proposed by the Abbé Groulx and his friends the germ of a movement for which he had little sympathy. From 1925 onwards he became more and more isolated in his own milieu. While English Canada continued to consider him a dangerous isolationist, he was more and more regarded by young French Canadians as a prophet who had stopped short of drawing the logical conclusion from his own political message. He had taught them liberty and self-respect. They began to consider that these words, translated into political language, meant sovereignty or nothing.

Realizing that he had had his day, Bourassa stepped down from the editorship of *Le Devoir* in 1932 and went into semi-retirement. He kept his seat in parliament until 1935, but then suffered an ignominious defeat at the hands of an obscure young lawyer the Liberals had pitted against him.

During the conscription crisis of the early 1940s, when French Canadians were again united as they have seldom been in the last century, Bourassa came out of his retreat to make vigorous speeches against conscription and the war policies of the King government. Again he found himself in deep communion with his compatriots. But he was too old now – and too detached – to try to derive any personal benefit from this victory. He went back to his retreat and, save for a few rather lukewarm appearances on behalf of the short-lived Bloc Populaire of Maxime Raymond and André Laurendeau, he spent the rest of his life reading and, as he often said, preparing for his ultimate meeting with his Creator.

Bourassa's name will long be revered by Canadians of all origins because he was, first and above all, a man of principle. Time and again he could have found a comfortable niche for himself in either of the leading parties of his time. He preferred to remain isolated. That he was not merely acting as an incorrigible individualist is attested by the permanence of the uncommitted nationalist sentiment in Quebec. His main achievement was the moulding of this rather inarticulate feeling into a permanent force in the political life of Canada.

At times it may appear that this force is becoming the captive of a party. Leaders like St. Laurent, Duplessis and even Lesage must all have shared that illusion. But events have proved that the nationalism Bourassa shaped can never be completely and permanently alienated in favour of any party. The paradox of Henri Bourassa is that he came too early to be heeded by the Canadians of his time and that his message, even if it were now accepted, would perhaps be inadequate to cope with the new nationalism of his own people.

This paradox is typical of great men of ideas. They launch dynamic movements that then follow unexpected courses. Bourassa's lot was to give life to a principle that the rest of Canada was tempted to forget, the right of a people to decide its own fate. The ultimate decision of his people might not be the one Bourassa envisioned. But French Canadians will always remember him as the man who kindled in them the flame of liberty.

# Emily Carr

1871-1945

She ranks as our greatest woman artist, if not our greatest artist. A completely original painter who belonged to no school but influenced many, she was born in Victoria where she spent most of her life. She studied art in San Francisco, London and Paris and for years, working without recognition, sketched the Indian villages and forests of her native province. Discouraged by public apathy she quit painting for fifteen years but returned to it after meeting Lawren Harris and other members of the Group of Seven. In 1941 her book *Klee Wyck* won the Governor-General's Award for non-fiction. It was followed by *The Book of Small*, *The House of All Sorts*, *Growing Pains*, *The Heart of a Peacock* and *Pause: a Sketch Book*, the last three published posthumously. Her paintings are represented in all the major Canadian collections.

# *The Laughing One*

*by* WILLIAM KILBOURN

Anyone who sees a totem pole now, or enters the giant rain forests of British Columbia, does so in some measure, whether he knows it or not, with the eyes and inner vision of Emily Carr. In her painting and writing she stamped her vision on what a visiting English artist told her as a girl was the "unpaintable" west coast. After a lifetime of obscurity, Emily Carr in her seventies was recognized at last as a painter and a writer, and quite possibly the most remarkable woman in Canadian history. Few people have ever had to struggle so hard to follow a vocation or have ever fought through to such triumphs of personal and artistic integrity.

The fifth daughter of a strict Victorian household, she was considered a family disgrace—especially after she showed her work on returning home from exhibiting in the most revolutionary show of pre-1914 Paris. Her painting was never mentioned at home. Schools in British Columbia where she had taught before her Paris trip refused to employ her. Her private pupils deserted her. She eventually had to keep a boarding house, where she cooked and scrubbed for a motley crew, mainly of decaying gentility and pretentious vagrants who treated her with pity or contempt and did not hide their disgust for her wild paintings crowded on the walls. In the back yard she kept a kennel of forty bobtail sheepdogs, which she raised to sell, and a kiln (which she often had to tend all night with a hose) to fire pottery for tourists. For most of her twenty-two years as a landlady she had little time to paint at all. Once she gave up painting entirely.

Rejection came early, and always for the same reason: her passion to tell the truth and to be entirely herself. It was a very young individualist who composed loud songs to the cow (to her older sisters' chagrin) or poured castor oil down the sad hen's throat (using her hostess's house as hospital); or once, overcome by joy on a forbidden picnic, fell into the sea. Before she was nine she saw it was not good for her father to be treated like God, and at the rebellion of his favourite he turned bitterly against her. When she was twelve her chief comfort disappeared with the death of her gentle and adored mother.

In the space and silence of the woods, Emily found healing and companionship in the old circus pony she rode there. Her love of animals was lifelong. Wild birds would readily fly to her hand. She once raised an abandoned vulture that walked to heel, and tamed to devotion a coon made vicious by cruelty. Many people knew her by her animals rather than her art. Some had dealings with them without knowing it. If she were out and the phone rang, Woo the monkey would let the parrot out of his cage and pick up the phone for him. "Hello," said the parrot. "Is Miss Carr there?" asked the caller. "And who else?" shrieked the parrot. "Speak up!" After crescendo hellos on both sides, Woo would get nervous and hang up, leaving the caller to wonder what sort of woman Miss Carr was.

She loved the Indians because they were honest about their feelings. When they were sad they cried, when they were happy they laughed. Their art showed essentials: "the part of the beaver that would still be beaver if he were skinned – his energy and courage, not the insignificant animal on our national emblem." She felt power in the simplicity of their totems many years before Picasso discovered the primitive, and she determined to record in paintings the carved poles that were rotting, so that Indians of the future would take pride in their heritage, and her countrymen better understand the culture they thought barbarous. Actually it was the Indians who were her first exhibitors and agents in the west, when the anthropologist Marius Barbeau saw her paintings in their houses. Through him the National Gallery first heard of her, though at fifty-six she had never heard of it.

Travelling alone by gas boat or fish-cannery ship, canoe and wagon to the remote villages, she battled mosquitoes with rancid bacon fat and turpentine, loneliness with a dog, and the endless rain by sheltering in half-roofed shacks or, once, in a shaman's grave. The Indians accepted and loved her, even in one village where missionaries and prospectors had been driven out with axes.

Her trip to Paris in 1910 took more courage than those up the wild coast. Crowded London a decade before had almost killed her; but she went because she felt the new language of forms being found in France could help her express the Canadian forest. Her work was always growing. Whether at forty or sixty, she was never too proud to be a student. One can see hints in her work of the liberating influences as they came; the volumes and movement of some of the cubist painters seen in France; the stark shapes of Lawren Harris after she had met the Group of Seven; the energy of the animated earth and sky of Van Gogh seen still later in Chicago; but always transformed and uniquely her own.

In the rain forests of the Pacific coast the undergrowth is a ten-foot wall and trees tower beyond practical proportion for painting. Perhaps it was the very difficulty of any literal approach to the landscape that drove her, more than painters in the east, to transform the outer world into a saga of the spirit. In her paintings, young growth dances irreverently at the feet of its elders. A tree, stripped of its fellows, rejected as useless by the loggers, is crowned and dazzled by the light of heaven. Green renewal bared to the sky thrusts over black and empty stumps. Each painting has the imprint of her own biography.

Winding through the serious purpose in her life, her sense of humour runs like a sparkling stream. The Indians saw it early and called her Klee Wyck, the laughing one. Laughter, especially at herself, was often the only cure for despair. She always kept diaries of humorous drawings to record her trips, her fatness, her sickness, her animals, and her friends. She was once a newspaper cartoonist. When confined to bed unable to paint she wrote of the past, the Indians and her childhood. The Toronto publisher William Clarke saw in her first unconventional manuscript the merit that won it a Governor-General's Award. (Another publisher had rejected it and then lost the only copy for a year.) Clarke encouraged her to send him a book every year. Her books first brought popular attention to her paintings. In 1941, Victoria gave her its approval with an official seventieth birthday party, and in her last years her work was shown in twenty-seven exhibitions in Europe and America.

The long struggle left its scars. She was formidably difficult, and quick to take offence where none was meant. The strategy of unaffected innocence and forthrightness with which she played the role of artist and woman in a philistine antifeminist society could itself be a little affected, at least in some of her writing. But at the centre of her life, and nowhere more than among the open and simple souls she befriended and protected with love and a sharp tongue, she lived in an essential condition of blessedness and truth. She once said she tried to paint "rhythm, sensed more than seen, making visible the shapes of awe in the human heart." Paint that rhythm she truly did. Everything we know of her was alive with its beat.

# Sir Thomas Chapais

1858-1946

His work in interpreting the wealth of their history to his French-Canadian compatriots helped lay the groundwork for the "quiet revolution." Born at St. Denis de Kamouraska, he was called to the Quebec bar in 1879. But he preferred journalism, scholarship and politics to law. From 1884 to 1901 he edited *Le Courrier du Canada* at Quebec. He was a professor of history at Laval during the same period. He served in the Legislative Council of Quebec and was a cabinet minister in three provincial governments. In 1919 he was appointed to the Canadian Senate, setting a precedent by being a member of two upper houses at the same time. But he is best known for his monumental histories, including studies of Jean Talon and the Marquis of Montcalm and an eight-volume history of Canada between 1760 and 1867.

# *The Interpreter*

*by MAURICE LEBEL*

Thomas Chapais was Canadian to the core. For over thirty years he was the French Canadian best able to set before an English-speaking audience the exact positions of the two founding races. He had the knack of saying plain truths to his listeners, and of convincing fair-minded people that his intentions were sound. As a gifted public orator, as an outstanding university professor and writer of Canadian history, as a faithful servant of the Crown both in Quebec and in Ottawa, he gave French Canadians historical and political reasons for reconciling themselves to living in a confederated Canada. His newspaper and review articles, his university lectures and his public speeches were widely studied in intellectual and political circles. In fact, a whole generation was brought up on his view of Canadian affairs. He was highly respected for his knowledge of universal history and his extremely lucid, precise and elegant prose; so highly respected, indeed, that he was honoured by Canada and knighted by France and Great Britain.

Both his father and his father-in-law were among the Fathers of Confederation. In 1867 his father took him for the first time to the new capital at Ottawa. Sir George Etienne Cartier, the political chieftain of French Canada and the Grand Trunk Railway's principal solicitor, travelled with them. To enliven the long journey he played a practical joke on the boy. While Thomas was pacing up and down the carriage, Cartier stole his bag of candies. Failing to find his travel vitamins when he sat down again, the boy flared up and began to call the statesman names. Cartier quickly reassured him by returning the candy and adding oranges. Thomas was never to see him again. But fifty years later, when the beautiful monument to Sir George was unveiled in Montreal, the orator was Thomas Chapais himself. He took advantage of the circumstance to apologize for his early impoliteness.

Chapais was sixteen when he delivered his maiden speech, at Collège Sainte-Anne-de-la-Pocatière, from which he graduated with highest honours two years later. Refusing to read from notes, he always memorized his addresses so perfectly that they passed for brilliant improvisations. But he never mastered his stage fright. His speeches make up several books. Many are among his handwritten manuscripts (during his long career, he never used a typewriter). At Laval University he studied law; he was called to the bar at twenty-one. On several memorable occasions he revealed an extremely sound legal mind, yet the practice of law never interested him; he preferred journalism. Soon after abandoning law for newspaper work he became editor and proprietor of *Le Courrier du Canada*, which he printed almost single-handed for seventeen years. His paper was a strong advocate of Confederation. Carried away by enthusiasm and temperament, he wrote several caustic articles against Laurier, whom he called "The Yankee" or "The Traitor." He thought Laurier was far too American. Chapais was for years the terror of the political press. He had also a lively sense of humour, which he exercised in the form of open letters to the federal government signed with the Greek pseudonym *Archilochus*. However bitter he might be in his attacks, he always expressed himself in such correct and elegant style that newspapermen held him in high esteem; he was the leading journalist of his time. But he was also preparing the ground for his later work as a historian; for twenty-two years he wrote in the *Revue Canadienne* a monthly review of national and international affairs.

His preoccupation with politics eventually convinced him that he should run for parliament. Happily, he was defeated; he was far too academic, polished and distant an orator for the electorate. This failure did not prevent him from remaining throughout his life a sound political adviser to party leaders, but it did turn out to be his intellectual salvation. After his electoral defeat he accepted, at thirty-four, a life membership in the Legislative Council at Quebec, where he kept his seat for fifty-four years. He was also, for twenty-seven years, a senator in Ottawa. These comfortable positions allowed him to carry on historical research and to devote his energy to writing.

For years he was Arthur Doughty's collaborator in the National Archives of Ottawa, never refusing his contribution to *Canada and its Provinces*. He wrote a biography, *Jean Talon*, which he translated himself into English under the title *The Great Intendant, A Chronicle of Jean Talon in Canada*; among his manuscripts, three volumes on the other eleven intendants of New France still await publication. He was widely read in English literature, and was inclined, with Carlyle, to consider biography to be the only true history. His second biography, *Le Marquis de Montcalm*, reveals his sure knowledge of the diplomatic history of the eighteenth century.

Chapais was more deeply steeped in the history of England than his predecessors and contemporaries in Quebec. For eighteen years he lectured in Canadian history at Laval University. The result of his teaching is embodied in his eight-volume *History of Canada*, which covers the century under British rule before Confederation. He stopped at 1867 because he thought that in view of his family and marriage relationships he would not have been as objective on the post-Confederation period as he had been in dealing with the century before it. He has often been rebuked by the so-called objective and scientific "nationalist" historians, less for being a Tory than for not being as anti-British as they would have liked. But his massive, carefully documented *History* tells more than their yappings; it is still a standard work.

Chapais was more than a pugnacious journalist, a brilliant academic orator, a highly conscientious and fair-minded historian. He was a writer with a deep love of Canadian history, and a rare insight into the shape of things to come. This short, thin, frail man felt at home in the dusty light of archives and churches. He lived so closely with books and the past that he asked to have his body lie in his own library, and be buried in his seventeenth-century domain. With his death, the curtain fell on an era that the young today hardly care to remember. Nevertheless his memorial will remain rooted in our language and in our conscience: the sharp clear prism of his intelligence and the clean pure breath of his soul.

# Sir Arthur Currie

1875-1933

By keeping the Canadian Corps intact as a fighting unit in World War I he helped to spark that growing sense of national identity which was a feature of postwar Canada. Born in Napperton, Ontario, he began his adult life as a schoolteacher and then as a real-estate salesman and executive in British Columbia. When the war broke out he was a lieutenant-colonel in the militia. In 1914 he was given command of a Highland battalion. By 1917 he was knighted and a lieutenant-general in charge of all Canadian troops in action. In 1919 he was made the first full general in Canadian history. From 1920 until his death he was principal and vice-chancellor of McGill University. He held seventeen honorary degrees.

# *The Civilian General*

*by Maj.-Gen. F. F. WORTHINGTON*

"Thine own reproach alone do fear." That is the motto on the Currie crest and is the precept by which I believe Sir Arthur lived, and on which his decisions, large and small, were made. The knowledge that eventually he would have to account to himself, and that it mattered, gave him the moral and physical courage to do what he believed necessary, cost him what it might. Certainly something gave him inner strength. His path was a difficult one, yet could have been smooth and far more materially rewarding had he chosen to compromise.

To my regret I never knew him well personally. Even in Canada's unconventional army there was a wide gap between corporal and corps commander, but we used to see him forward in the battle zone inspecting conditions for himself and making his own reconnaissance. Critics have called him cold and austere; to me at that time he appeared more like a man deep in profound thought. Certainly his associates never found him cold. They respected and admired him as did his staff, who had to have active service at the front before he would take them on. But Canadian Corps Headquarters was no ivory tower.

Originals of the First Division, and there were not many left, were devoted to "Barrage" Currie, a name they gave him because of his insistence on firepower to protect his manpower. To the rest of us the First Division had a special aura, having been Currie's division and setting the standard and pace for other Canadian divisions to live up to.

My feeling about Currie is that he was made for the time and the time made for him. Under him the Canadian Corps developed a genuine pride in *being* Canadian, outgrowing the prevalent acceptance of colonialism. Even I, who had spent less than a month in Canada – where I went to enlist – felt it and became ardently "Canadian."

He was thirty-nine when the war broke out and he was ordered to Valcartier to command the Second Infantry Brigade of the First Division. In less than three years he was in command of the Canadian Army in the field; by the end of the war he was recognized as one of the outstanding generals on the Western Front. Lloyd George seriously considered making him commander-in-chief had he been able to get rid of Haig. In this astonishing rise Currie was in competition with the best British military men of the time, but the marvel is that he had no political pull. In fact, the reverse was the case; he succeeded in spite of fanatical opposition from Canadians in England and at home. He held no brief for political manoeuvring. When he was approached in 1918 to "consider a stand returned soldiers should take after the war," he replied, "I do not propose to associate myself with the schemes of any set of soldier-politicians."

Currie's rudimentary militia training may have been the secret of his success. He had learned basic military principles, but his mind was not cluttered with orthodoxy and dogma, which can smother initiative. He had the courage and intelligence to maintain independence of thought and action, and he was not wedded to ideas conceived and employed over the past century. With an open mind he listened to clever men around him, considered their opinions, wise and otherwise, saw reason in radicalism and tested it out. He made mistakes but, unlike many, he learned from them. His goal was to beat the Germans with the smallest possible sacrifice of his own men. Soldiers in the line became mindful of this, and by triggering their enthusiasm he made up for his lack of flamboyance. By the time he took command of the Corps his reputation was known, and it instilled confidence in all.

Even though he fell foul of the British high command because of his blunt refusals to commit his command piecemeal or without adequate preparation, in the end he earned Haig's respect as a general who could win battles.

Ironically, needless slaughter for his own aggrandizement was the sin for which Canadians at home crucified him. At the end of the war and Canada's triumphant "Hundred Days," Sir Arthur wrote to Prime Minister Sir Robert Borden: "It has been intimated to me that a section of the American press is seeking to belittle the work of Canadians, intimating that what we call 'Imperial troops' have done the bulk of the fighting . . . I am inclined to think that the English press are the people to blame . . . their reports on operations since August 8th (1918) have in very few cases been fair or just to Canadians . . . Certain sections of the English press are evidently determined on a policy to ignore the word 'Canadian' . . . and I believe the papers receive their instructions from the highest military authorities . . . Our own papers in Canada republish the English articles . . . and the Canadian people do not even now realize the full extent of the (Corps') operation . . . and many think the casualties have been unduly heavy."

But those in Canada who knew the facts did nothing to refute these accusations. Sam Hughes, in speeches in the House of Commons, deliberately fostered them.

Back in Canada after the war, Currie served only briefly as inspector-general, but he continued to support the Non-Permanent Active Militia, believing in Canada's ultimate need for it. In a Canadian Club address in 1926 he expressed the same idea President John F. Kennedy put forward in his inaugural address thirty-five years later. "We must think," Sir Arthur said, "not of the militia and what it needs from Canada, but of Canada and what she needs from the militia."

My own association with Currie began later, when he was principal and vice-chancellor of McGill University. I was in the militia at the time, and was put in charge of the arrangements for a dance of which Sir Arthur and Lady Currie were patrons. My life had been lived in the rough and tumble of tramp ships and the army, so that my knowledge of the social graces was limited. A lesser man than Currie would have been indignant at my bumbling; I think he was quietly amused. Anyway he made a friend for life.

In 1928 he brought a libel action against a newspaper in Port Hope, Ontario, against the advice of his friends. He had borne insinuations of cowardice and callousness for nearly ten years. Now the accusation was in the open and he felt constrained to clear his name for the sake of his family, fearful of their suffering and the consequent self-reproach time might bring him. Though he won the case the victory was a hollow one. The trial was a mockery of fair play, for the great weight of public opinion was still implacably against him. But on his return from the trial to Montreal, Windsor Station and the streets leading to McGill University were packed with cheering veterans and undergraduates who knew the man.

Throughout his life Sir Arthur Currie remained true to his principles. Now he is taking his rightful place in Canada's history, an honoured one. His enemies are lost in anonymity – too good for them, but Currie was not a vindictive man.

# Clennell H. "Punch" Dickins

1899-

His name is synonymous with bush flying and northern exploration. Born at Portage La Prairie, Manitoba, and educated at the University of Alberta, he became a World War I air ace (he won the DFC) and later a pioneer northern pilot. He was an executive of the old Canadian Airways, first in the Mackenzie River district (where he made several record-breaking flights into new areas) and later in Winnipeg, where from 1935 to 1940 he served as general superintendent. In 1928 he received the McKee Trophy for pioneering in the air. During the war he organized the Atlantic Ferry Service and then served as general manager of Canadian Pacific Airlines before moving, in 1947, to de Havilland Aircraft of Canada, where he is now executive vice-president.

# *The Sky Explorer*

Back in the late 1920s, when I was going to high school in Edmonton, there was only one kind of hero for any red-blooded youth to acknowledge. He wasn't a movie star or even a soldier of fortune, though he combined the glamour of one and the daring of the other. It was the new breed of bush pilot that we worshipped–and with good reason, for Edmonton was the jumping-off place for most bush pilots. Off they hopped, from our very midst, fur-clad and clear of eye into a dangerous, frozen and uncharted land. They were opening up the last frontier and their names were on everybody's lips–names like Wop May, Leigh Brintnell, Matt Berry, Stan McMillan, Con Farrell, Harry Hayter, Archie McMullen, Cy Becker, Vic Horner, Bob Randall . . .

. . . and of course "Punch" Dickins. Clennell H. Dickins–though few called him anything but Punch. More than any of the others he symbolizes the bush pilot to me.

By the time I was ready to become a bush pilot myself (I chose the neighbouring Yukon) Dickins had a series of awesome achievements behind him. He had launched the first airmail service across the prairies. He had become the first human being to fly across the unmapped barrenlands. He had flown the first airmail to the coast of the Arctic Sea. Now he was in charge of the Mackenzie district for Canadian Airways, which was fighting a tooth-and-nail battle with its rival, Mackenzie Air Services.

I can still remember him as he looked then: Hollywood's idea of a bush pilot, straight out of Central Casting . . . supple, hard frame, trimmed of all fat . . . jet black hair, tightly crew-cut, the face of a small, eager boy. He made a fetish of precision. His fellows might dress sloppily in

*by* GRANT McCONACHIE

rumpled jackets and trousers but Dickins in his brown deerskin jacket with matching breeches, his high-topped leather boots, his freshly laundered flannel shirt and his leather gloves was positively immaculate. In the winter he chose Eskimo garb – fur parka and mukluks. His great fur gauntlets were made to his own specifications.

This precision carried over to his aircraft, and may well have been his most precious asset in that unforgiving wilderness north of fifty-eight. I suspect the black-gang of mechanics thought him something of a martinet, for he insisted that his plane be gleaming, pin-neat and tuned to perfection at all times. This may be one reason why he is alive and kicking today.

I knew him well in each of his several lively careers. During that first career of bush flying from 1927 to 1939 he covered eight hundred thousand miles, mostly in unmapped northern country and often in temperatures that nudged fifty below. Remember the conditions: no radio link with civilization; no chance to signal for help if forced down; only his own ingenuity to keep him alive when a blizzard grounded him and his passengers. It was Dickins who had to make camp in the howling snow and keep himself and his charges warm, fed and healthy.

He had few accidents. There was one I remember at Fort Fitzgerald. The shrieking gales had moulded the snowdrifts hard as granite. When Punch landed, the legs of his ski undercarriage snapped and both his propeller tips were hopelessly bent. He and his engineer, Lew Parmenter, made new ski struts out of some discarded metal pipes and then hacksawed six inches off the prop ends. They successfully flew the crippled plane home for repairs. But the most memorable flight of Punch Dickins was, of course, that great trip he made across the barrenlands. He had five hundred unexplored and unmapped miles to traverse, from Baker Lake on the east to Athabasca on the west. His compass was rendered virtually useless by the proximity of the magnetic pole. And the land below had a sameness about it that must have been maddening: featureless tundra stretching for hundreds of miles to all horizons . . . ridge after identical ridge left by the receding glaciers . . . tattered, unknown lakes, each indistinguishable from the others. Yet Punch Dickins found his way across this empty desert, then flew on to Fort Smith and doubled back all the way to Winnipeg. Until that moment, the journey was one that would have taken two years of hazardous travel. Dickins covered four thousand miles of wilderness in just thirty-eight flying hours spread over eleven days. He had dramatized for the world the value of the bush plane.

He had a knack of being around when history was made. There was the sunny afternoon in October, 1929, when he was flying a prospector along the east shore of Great Bear Lake, where the cliffs rise a sheer five hundred feet from the navy-blue waters. Suddenly the passenger exclaimed over a technicolor island, glowing purple and yellow in the afternoon sun.

The passenger, of course, was Gilbert LaBine. The colours that excited him were mineral oxides suggesting pitchblendes. It was this flight that led to the historic Eldorado Mine–the discovery that broke the world monopoly on radium and helped usher in the nuclear age.

It seems to me that, of all those pioneer flyers, Dickins stands alone. It is not merely that he survived. Nor is it only the dazzling succession of early achievements that sets him apart. More than the others, Dickins progressed. One might call him the Picasso of bush pilots since he was never content with one career. He moved along with the air age and he is as much a part of it today as he was in the 1920s.

I knew Dickins best between 1942 and 1947, when we were closely associated in the gangling adolescence of Canadian Pacific Airlines. He had already completed a second career, organizing and operating for Canadian Pacific the Atlantic Ferry Service, later handed over to the RAF. This was the operation that set the pattern for Canada's postwar ventures in over-ocean air transport. Now we had acquired ten money-losing bush operations and it was Punch Dickins's job as vice-president and general manager to make sense out of a conglomeration that included seventy-seven aircraft of fourteen varieties scattered all across the north and all flying in the red.

It was a nightmarish assignment. But from those often frustrating years, Dickins emerged as the world authority on bush flying and on the shortcomings of existing bush aircraft. It was no surprise to me when de Havilland of Canada hired him to help create the ideal bushplane.

Today this aircraft–the Beaver–carries Canada's name around the world. Punch Dickins is its father. He insisted on all-metal construction, big loading-doors, high power-weight ratio, and short take-off performance. So successful was this all-Canadian aircraft that the U.S. Forces bought a thousand. Another six hundred were sold to customers all over the globe. With Dickins's know-how, de Havilland created a major Canadian export industry, for bigger and better planes were to follow–the Otter, Caribou and Buffalo–all arising out of the Canadian environment.

Dickins today is executive vice-president of de Havilland but he doesn't really look or act like one. For one thing, he never seems to age: the boyish, matinee-idol look is still there, perhaps because the boyish enthusiasm for flying is still there. Dickins has no hobbies because he needs none: flying is his life. I doubt if he likes to be called an executive, for he has said he prefers an earlier and nobler title. They gave him an honorary degree not long ago and he put it into words then: "I'm proud of the title 'bush pilot'," he said. "It originated in Canada, it relates to men of dedicated interest in flying to the remote regions and I hope it will never disappear."

# Timothy Eaton

1834-1907

He revolutionized the commercial world of his time. Born a farmer's son in County Antrim, Ireland, he came to Canada in 1854 and, with his two elder brothers, ran a general store at St. Mary's, Upper Canada. In 1868 he moved to Toronto and entered the dry-goods business. The following year he founded the family company that bears his name, selling for cash at a fixed price–two practices which were then unknown. Thus did he build one of the largest family-owned businesses in the world and make of the Eaton's catalogue a genuine Canadian artifact.

# *The Radical Storekeeper*

*by* *ARTHUR HAILEY*

When poets and politicians are long forgotten, the name of Timothy Eaton is likely to endure.

He was an Irish farm boy who became a Canadian immigrant and, later, one of the great world merchants of his era. More significantly, he revolutionized the methods and ethics of retail selling, so that even now, more than half a century after his death, Timothy Eaton's ideas and influence still pervade our scene.

The inner personality of the founder of Eaton's of Canada was, and still is, largely a mystery. He committed few of his thoughts to paper. He made no public speeches. His politics were undefined. Biographies written after his death give an impression of the influential Eaton family peering over writers' shoulders–the result, a vanity-press mixture of politeness and awe.

Despite this cautious filtering, there are hints that Timothy Eaton was often dour and frequently arbitrary. He appears to have been a serious man with no strong sense of humour. Though he understood salesmanship, he was not a good salesman himself, his manner being abrupt. He held strict religious views, opposed liquor and smoking, and would not allow card playing or dancing in his house. To this day no Eaton store sells tobacco or cigarettes, and in Eaton display windows the drapes are down on Sundays. He detested unions, and a disgruntled employee once wrote, "He was very much against Labour Day and would fire anyone who looked out the window at the parade."

Yet viewed in the context of his time, Timothy Eaton was a progressive liberal. Defying sceptics and competitors, he set new standards of honest dealing with the public. He was considerate of employees and gave, unasked, concessions for which unions elsewhere fought bitter battles. For all his arbitrariness, he seems essentially to have been a kind man. And despite the firmness of his views, throughout his life his mind was consistently open to new ideas.

This was apparent even at the opening of the original Eaton store, a tiny shop at the southwest corner of Yonge and Queen Streets in Toronto. On a bitterly cold December day in 1869, a small advertisement in the Toronto *Globe* proclaimed, "New Dry Goods Business!" T. Eaton & Co. offered "staple haberdashery, sound goods, staples and flannels." But more startling was the statement: "We propose to sell our goods for CASH only–in selling goods we have only one price."

This was unprecedented. In 1869 barter was still a normal means of trade in the countryside, and even in cities haggling was the rule. A direct exchange of cash was considered crude. Eaton believed this kind of commerce to be unfair to both customers and merchants. Customers who were not shrewd traders got the poorest deals, and merchants were frequently saddled with bartered items for which there was no demand. The new store pursued a simple, consistent policy: the sale of quality articles at the lowest possible prices that would allow a fair profit for the retailer.

Experienced merchants predicted early disaster. They scoffed even more when the crazy Irishman made his now-famous pledge: Goods Satisfactory or Money Refunded. No business, they predicted, could survive such conditions. But goodwill based on fair dealing grew and grew, and so did Eaton's.

Though a grandson, John David Eaton, now heads the mammoth, nation-wide chain of Eaton stores, the founder's original policies are followed consistently today. Advertising is an example. For many years Timothy Eaton wrote his own, observing a simple rule: advertisements must tell the truth. Eventually the growth of business made an advertising department necessary. Typically, Timothy Eaton issued a directive–handwritten on a scrap of paper–which is still preserved and honoured. "Tell your story to public–what you have and what you propose to sell. Promise them . . . every article will be found just what it is guaranteed to be. Use no deception in the smallest degree."

Timothy Eaton set the pattern of innovation. His store tested and introduced many firsts; when the first passenger elevator was installed, wax figures rode up and down before customers could be induced to try it. He developed catalogue shopping and Eaton's own manufacturing facilities. He was receptive to the ideas of others and would listen to argument, then sometimes reverse an earlier judgment. It is recorded that he resisted purchase of a typewriter but when confronted with a batch of letters for signature, neatly typed, adopted the machine enthusiastically.

He was a pioneer of fair labour practices. Remembering the hardships of his apprentice years in Ireland, where he worked from five in the morning to midnight, he determined that his employees should have time for rest and recreation. Soon after setting up in business he began closing his store at eight in the evening, two hours earlier than competitors. By 1880 closing was at six o'clock, except on Saturday. Later Timothy Eaton proposed Saturday afternoon closing during summer. He invited customers to vote on the idea, but the majority was opposed. Characteristically, he went ahead anyway–closing at two on Saturday afternoons during July and August. Through most of his career, no employee worked harder than he. A biography records, "Oftentimes at night he went home and threw himself on the lounge utterly exhausted–too tired even to take his supper."

His personal life was touched by tragedy. His father died before Timothy's birth. Though Timothy Eaton's marriage to Margaret Beattie was lasting and happy, three of their eight children died in infancy, one by drowning. Their eldest son Edward–his father's pride and heir apparent–died of diabetes at thirty-seven.

Timothy Eaton died in 1907 at seventy-two. The Toronto *Globe* observed, "He was beyond the skyline of mere trade and had a care for the worth and dignity of life."

# Sir Sandford Fleming

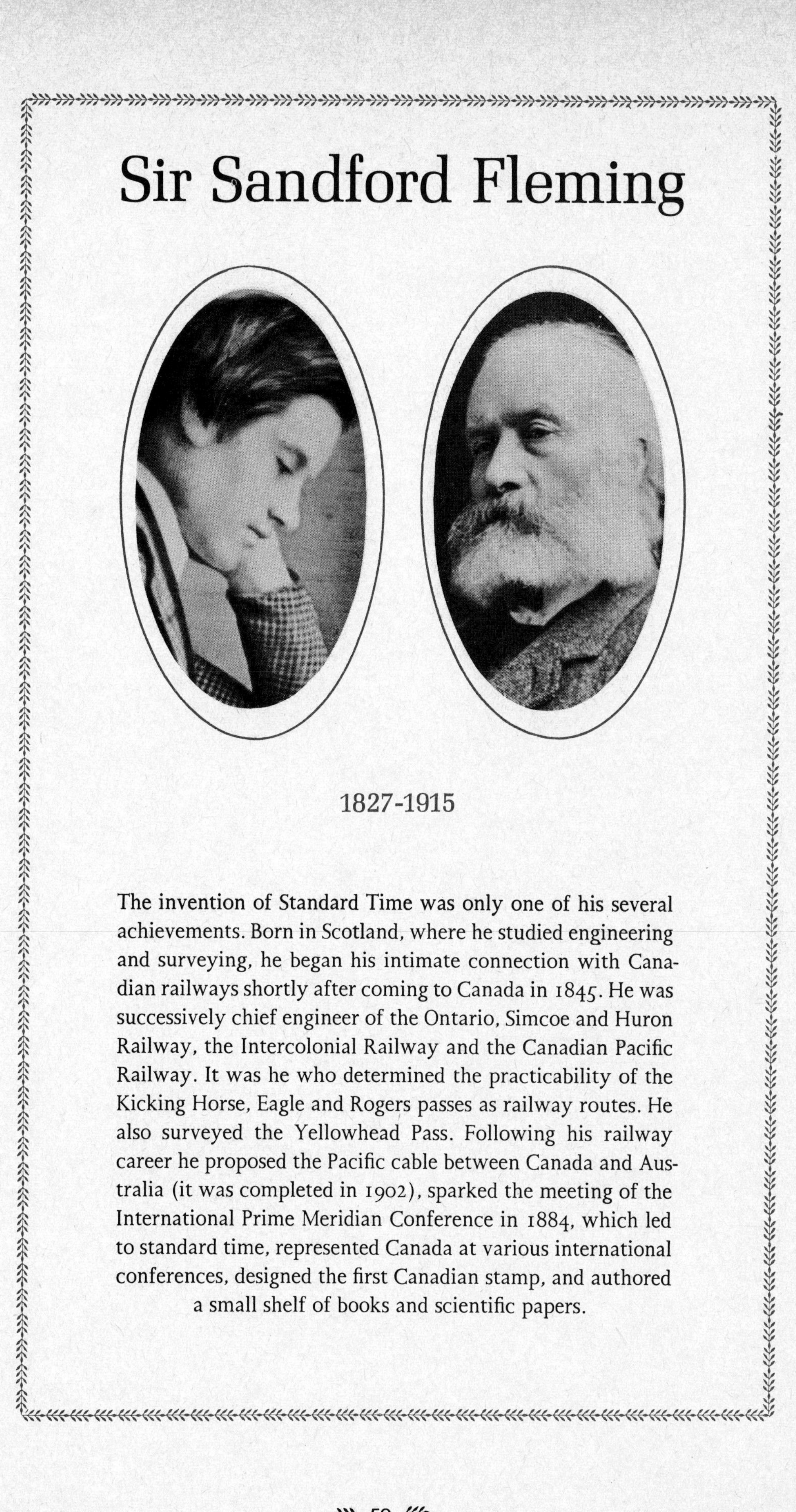

1827-1915

The invention of Standard Time was only one of his several achievements. Born in Scotland, where he studied engineering and surveying, he began his intimate connection with Canadian railways shortly after coming to Canada in 1845. He was successively chief engineer of the Ontario, Simcoe and Huron Railway, the Intercolonial Railway and the Canadian Pacific Railway. It was he who determined the practicability of the Kicking Horse, Eagle and Rogers passes as railway routes. He also surveyed the Yellowhead Pass. Following his railway career he proposed the Pacific cable between Canada and Australia (it was completed in 1902), sparked the meeting of the International Prime Meridian Conference in 1884, which led to standard time, represented Canada at various international conferences, designed the first Canadian stamp, and authored a small shelf of books and scientific papers.

# *The Renaissance Man*

*by* HARRY BRUCE

The awful physical challenges of nineteenth-century Canada bred a style of man that grew nowhere else in the world and, now, has died out even here. He was the Renaissance Man of the Wilderness. He was a scientist, a philanthropist, a gentleman scholar, a man of public affairs, an unswerving churchman and perhaps a poetry-lover and after-supper painter, as well; at the same time, he was as hard as the blade of a voyageur's axe, and second only to the Indian at scratching a living out of a wild and ungenerous land. The Renaissance Man of the Wilderness was the link between Alexander Mackenzie and the board rooms and the city streets and universities of twentieth-century Canada and, if he was tough enough and cheerful enough, he could enjoy both worlds in a way that has never been open to any other group of Canadians.

The toughest, noblest and most accomplished of these strong-minded men was the railroad-builder, Sir Sandford Fleming. Sir Andrew Macphail

once said that it was just possible Fleming was not the greatest engineer who ever lived; he was merely "the greatest man who ever concerned himself with engineering."

Fleming lived to be eighty-eight and during his seventy years in Canada he pursued an incredible variety of engineering passions and public interests. They took him from Kicking Horse Pass to a night at the opera with the Prince of Wales. He spent the evening of his twenty-fourth birthday sleeping with a dozen Indians on the banks of Lake Huron in three feet of snow and a wind that pushed the temperature down to fourteen below; he spent later birthdays on the other side of the world, with prime ministers and royalty. He crossed Canada by foot, snowshoe, dog team, canoe, wagon, raft and dug-out log–and he did it more than once. In the heart of one brutal winter he drove in a sleigh more than three hundred miles–between Shediac, New Brunswick, and Rimouski, Quebec–in five days. But he also cruised Venice in a gondola, went up in a balloon in Paris and, to advance his scheme for a state-owned British Empire cable system, he visited five continents by steamer.

Once, somewhere on the trail of a future railroad, Fleming pulled a wolfskin over his head and joined a mob of dancing Indians. He also threw lusty parties of his own, in Ottawa and Halifax, and his guests included almost all the powerful Canadians of his long era, and most of the governors-general of Canada. Moreover, according to Sir Andrew Macphail, "he met and knew intimately every personage of note in the Empire." Once, he routed a large bear that was blocking his path in a desolate part of Ontario; he did it with nothing more than an umbrella and some shouting. Half a century later, he routed private telegraph interests in Britain, who were blocking his plan for a government cable linking Canada to Australia. His weapons for that job were twenty years of Scottish tenacity, plenty of his own dollars and what Earl Grey described as the missionary fervour of St. Paul. (The cable was laid in 1902.)

Fleming is best known as the man who devised a workable system of Standard Time, and did more than anyone else to promote its use around the world. A paper he wrote about Standard Time in 1876 suggests the kind of scholarship one expects from really sound Renaissance Men of the Wilderness. Fleming talks, with considerable dash, not merely about time-keeping systems of contemporary Poles, Chinese, Bohemians, Italians, Japanese, Arabians, Jews and Turks, but also about time-keeping among most of the ancient Mediterranean peoples.

Fleming's importance to Canadian history, however, stems neither from cables nor clocks, but from railroads. He was the man who *worked* on the railroads while the politicians and the promoters merely talked about them. He surveyed the routes and built the track over a great part of the Canadian railroad system that finally linked the Atlantic to the Pacific. In its time, the system was an astonishing engineering triumph. Fleming was so obviously superior to any other railroad engineer in Canada that, for a while, he held down no fewer than three of the biggest railway jobs in the country: he was chief engineer for the Intercolonial Railway, which was under construction between Halifax and Quebec; chief engineer for the Canadian Pacific Railway, for which he was to survey the route west from Ontario to the Pacific; and chief engineer of the survey for what would one day be the Newfoundland Railway. "No man without his extraordinary mental and physical vigour could have borne the tremendous strain," his friend and biographer, L. J. Burpee, wrote. "The task was Herculean."

Fleming was deeply respected wherever engineers met, but not only for his great technical abilities. When, in 1880, he became chancellor of Queen's University, he told his diary: "This is the strangest thing of my life. What made them elect a man to the highest position, who has never been in his life at college?" He was, perhaps, too genuinely modest to appreciate that the best reason Queen's could possibly have for naming him chancellor was his own reputation for integrity. As Sir Andrew Macphail wrote many years after Fleming's death, "his hands were clean, his eye was single, his heart was pure." And, from one end of his railroads to the other, Canadians knew it.

# Gratien Gélinas

1909-

As "Fridolin" he made home-grown theatre a smashing commercial and critical success in French Canada. Playwright, director, producer and actor all rolled into one, he staged cabaret sketches so successfully that he was able to quit the insurance business in 1937 and devote himself full time to his art. Well known to radio and television audiences, he is perhaps best known among English-speaking Canadians for his play *Tit Coq* (Little Rooster) which toured several Canadian cities and was seen briefly on Broadway, and for *Bousille et les Justes*. Born at St. Tite, near Trois-Rivières, of a French-Canadian father and a Scots-Irish mother, he holds two honorary degrees and has been showered with a host of other honours, not the least of which is the audience's continued and enthusiastic applause.

# *The Showman*

*by* KEN LEFOLII

The first time Gratien Gélinas spoke English on the stage was in 1945, when he played a character role in a potboiler intended to revive the fame of a forgotten star named Miriam Hopkins. The play closed in Chicago, where the critics advised Miss Hopkins to stay forgotten. While it lasted, though, the same critics made Gélinas the toast of the town. They called him, among other things, "one of the great talents of our contemporary stage," and compared him to Charlie Chaplin. Since then every Canadian who has written at any length about Gélinas, including me, has described him as the Chaplin of Canada. The phrase now seems to me to have the witless quality of a Moose Jaw politician trying to campaign like a Kennedy, and to conform to the same uncomfortable axiom: When an American drops a cliché, two or more Canadians will bend over and pick it up. I am sorry about my part in fielding this one, because Gélinas deserves better.

The Charlie Chaplin of the silver screen was a funny man in more ways than one; it is hard to imagine a more accomplished mimic or a more banal writer. Whatever similarities there may be between Chaplin and Gélinas as actors, as writers they are no more alike than Walt Disney and Stephen Leacock. Charlie the Tramp is invincible – like Donald the Duck, he is impervious to the human condition. But the little man Gratien Gélinas has spent most of his life developing on the stage is something else again. He is, God help him, one of us.

He has appeared under three names: Fridolin in the 1930s and '40s, Tit-Coq in the 1950s, and Bousille at the beginning of the 1960s. Unlike most of us, he has been a good man and a simple one, which is to say that he has been even more vulnerable to the human condition than we are. The plump people have naturally worked him over. They have put him down for being born a bastard, and for being too poor to buy them off. They have used his religion against him, in the name of their own priestly superstitions. They have brutalized him. In the end he has gone under, as people do. He is no hero. He is not even a fashionable contemporary antihero. He is just a decent little man.

Gélinas writes mainly with his ear and his mouth, using a tape recorder more often than a typewriter, and his lines are clear and straight. There are almost no memorable speeches in his plays. Nor are there any of the dislocations of sense and the technical stunt-jumping that make exercises in algebra out of many "modern" plays. The audience at a performance of *Tit-Coq* or *Bousille et les Justes* is watching a show; Gélinas is shooting for the stomach. I have seen *Bousille* three times, and each time a visible shudder of sick fear has run through the audience when Henri has twisted Bousille's bad knee backwards. What the creeps are doing to Bousille they are doing to you and me. He makes himself felt.

To last, this is the first thing a piece of writing has to do; squeeze an abstraction down into one man's head and stomach. Two bodies of Canadian writing have done this hard thing particularly well, Morley Callaghan's short stories and Gratien Gélinas's plays. My guess is that if any Canadian writing will last, they will.

For Callaghan and Gélinas themselves, the result of doing good work has been curiously reversed. Callaghan had the devotion of many intellectuals even before his work got the nod from Edmund Wilson, but the middlebrows have always been indifferent to his books, and the consequent sluggishness of the market has forced Callaghan to scramble for a living most of his adult life. Gélinas has had almost no serious attention from the aesthetes, partly, I suspect, because the middlebrows love him. He is spectacular, a genuine virtuoso: promoter, producer, director, actor, designer, writer. "Gélinas is that rare thing, an artist who knows the score," a Montreal critic once said of him; he may be the only theatrical personality in history who has owned one hundred percent of himself most of his life, and made it pay. By 1948 he was already reported to be earning seventy-five thousand dollars a year, net; *Tit-Coq* and *Bousille et les Justes* are the only genuine hits, in the Broadway sense, ever written and staged by a Canadian; a brewery has thought so highly of his acumen that it has spent several hundred thousand dollars to provide him with a permanent theatre in Montreal; the eminent businessmen on the board of *l'Université de Montréal* have given him the businessman's accolade, an honorary doctorate.

The trouble with all this, if there is one, is that Gélinas has done far too many things too well. In his late fifties his permanent work amounts to two plays and a movie version of *Tit-Coq*. He is too good to leave so little, but he has been too busy to write more. (He writes hard, shutting himself up for months in his country place at Oka and sleeping in twenty-minute snatches, often on the floor.)

Every time I have talked to him, he has spoken of making new movies. I hope he does. It is a pleasure to sit and watch what happens on that carroty little man's face, a face as long and deeply ploughed as a St. Lawrence strip-farm. It is a greater pleasure to listen to the queer, open way the little man has of saying how things really are with us these days. He could leave a lot of laughter in a can of film.

# Alain Grandbois

1900-

The dean of French-Canadian poets was born at Saint-Casimir de Portneuf, Quebec. His writing career began twenty-two years later in Paris, from which base he travelled to most of the continents of the world. His first prose work appeared in Paris in 1933, his first book of poetry in Hankow in 1934. (All but one of the privately printed copies were lost in a shipwreck.) In 1936 he enlisted on the Republican side in the Spanish Civil War, returning to Canada shortly before World War II to publish three books of poems that made his reputation. His collected works appeared in 1963. That same year he was named, with Donald Creighton, the first winner of a major world literary award – the Molson Prize. He now makes his home in Quebec City.

# *The Lonely Traveller*

*by MARCEL DUBE*

Alain Grandbois is a true poet. He lives as a citizen of the world and writes of the great and enduring themes that are above politics and beyond local jurisdictions–life, death, and love.

Twice, quite by chance, I have been able to have long conversations with him. There was first that winter night when I took the seat at his side on the train from Montreal to Mont-Rolland in the Laurentians. We spoke mainly of the French-Canadian literature that is developing now, and from this conversation I retain the memory of a pleasant hour in the company of a courteous and restless man. A few years later we found ourselves together in the parlour car of the Montreal-Quebec train (Grandbois lives near Quebec City). Everything about this conversation was different, even the poet's appearance. He had always been thin; now his face was emaciated. The evening before, a malaria attack in his hotel-room had almost finished him. He explained in a cold, precise manner just what malaria is. He smoked feverishly, without stop, raising his arm now and then for the bar steward. I questioned him. Slowly, with great clarity, giving the proper emphasis to meaningful details, and in a slightly broken voice, he recounted a little of his past. It was like a memory moving through a dark country under an empty sky at that time in April when the world waits desperately for spring. His eyes moved constantly from my face to the windows, from the attentive man at his side to the desolate landscape rushing past outside. We were strangers and friends; he spoke to me, but he was really questioning himself with grievous tenacity about the mystery of man's exile on earth.

The circumstances of these two meetings were almost poetically fitting, I have thought since. We met on trains running through the night. Grandbois's life has been a journey through the world, and his work has been a chart of man's journey toward death. For me he will always be the traveller with the lonely face.

He was born in the first hours of the twentieth century. He was trained to be a lawyer, he aspired to be a painter, he became a poet. But the truth about imagination is more often found in dreams than facts, and in his imagination Grandbois was already a traveller; he dreamed of voyaging on the sea.

"I should have been a sailor!" he once wrote in an autobiographical note. "My grandfather, Michel Grandbois, sailed to Australia when he was eighteen; he came back seven years later with a fortune. He told me stories of his adventures – stories of pirates! When he died he left me a special legacy, so that I could afford to travel and begin to understand things like pirates. I made expeditions, I explored. I used to like taking serious risks."

He went to Europe, then penetrated Africa and Asia. Even his books have an adventurous history: his second, *Poems*, was published in China in 1934, and every copy except one, which Grandbois has, was lost in a shipwreck. Some writers have suggested that Grandbois travelled to get material for his books. On the contrary; he travelled to reach far places, to go to the hearts of mysterious and ancient continents and there fulfil his marvellous imagination. He knew *how* to see the world, its landscapes and cities and peoples; he brought with him an insatiable thirst for experience. He did not travel to write. He travelled to live, and wrote later.

He will set a story on the Mediterranean coast, a poem in Africa. He is concerned with justice; with the conflict between individual freedom and the regimentation imposed by society; with love as the only possible way to try, at least, to cheat the law of death; and finally, always, with death itself. This preoccupation is sometimes held against him, as is the ironic detachment – some writers say arrogance – with which he looks at the masses of people who have given up their freedoms under the modern pressure to conform. I think, myself, that there is some critical confusion here: Grandbois has had the toughness of mind to stay outside a society he dislikes, and it is by looking on from the outside that he maintains his own dignity. It is a lonely position he has chosen, but one that commands respect.

Partly for this reason, Grandbois seems to me a true poet. He is trying to describe the angel whose ghost dwells in man and devours him from within, the fallen angel who invents heavens impossible to attain. Grandbois has no pity for human beings, but having searched their faces and listened to their speeches, having weighed their despair and examined their hope, he holds out to them, with a kind of modesty that verges on eloquence, a compassion that is not counterfeit. He sees in them what he sees in himself.

His manner in writing is grave, patient, careful to find words that will be simple and right. It is the work of an illuminator; a man who feels himself accountable to no one but himself and his own pleasure in his craft. There is in it courtesy, elegance, and a way of carefully passing on things that he acquired carefully. The number of paragraphs or volumes he leaves behind is not Grandbois's first concern, and I will never be able to share the opinion of those who condemn him for not having written more.

For one evening, one evening in April aboard the Montreal-Quebec train, I suddenly understood, in trying to follow the lively thread of his dreams, that this man had paid a great price for his loves.

# George Monro Grant

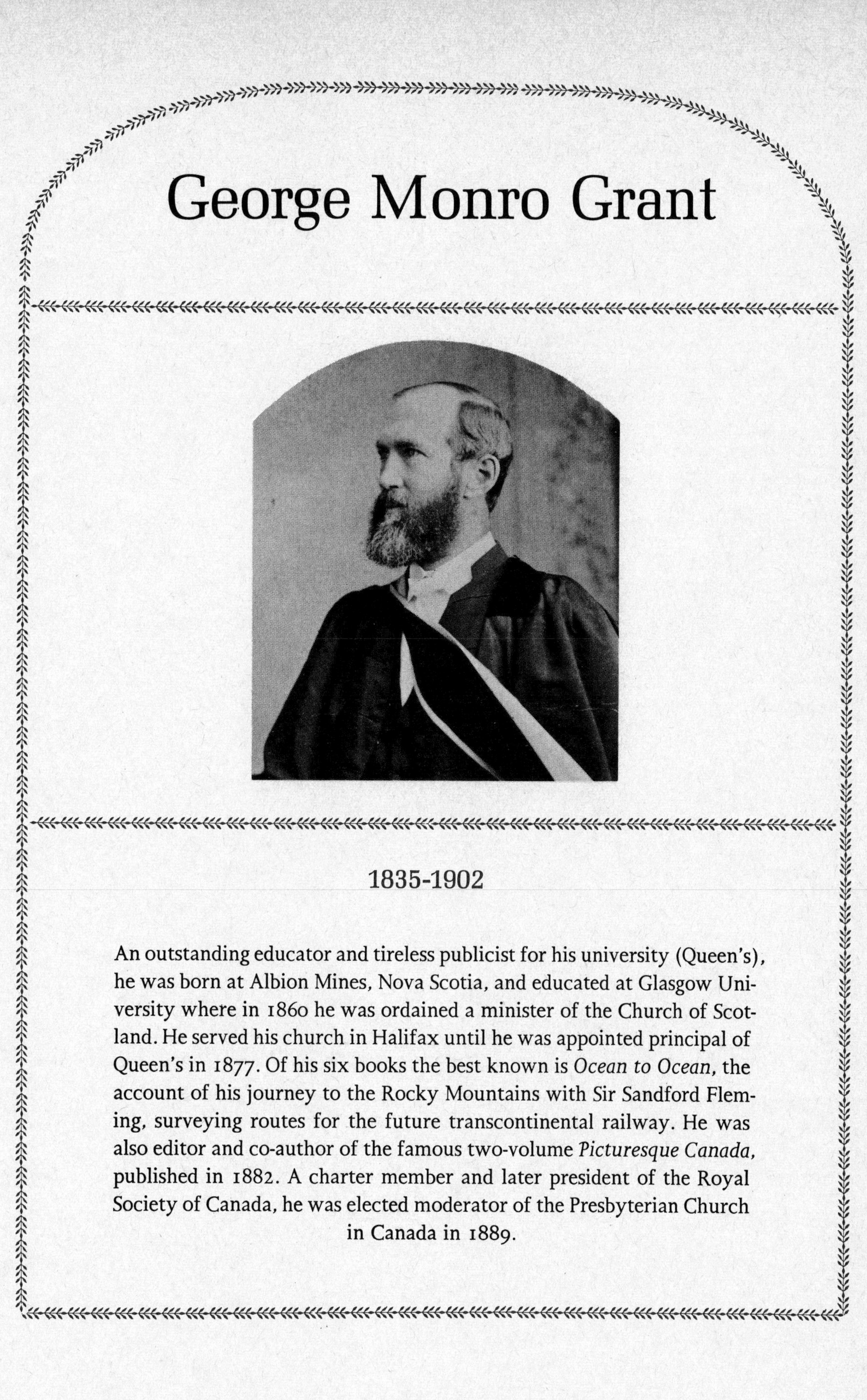

1835-1902

An outstanding educator and tireless publicist for his university (Queen's), he was born at Albion Mines, Nova Scotia, and educated at Glasgow University where in 1860 he was ordained a minister of the Church of Scotland. He served his church in Halifax until he was appointed principal of Queen's in 1877. Of his six books the best known is *Ocean to Ocean*, the account of his journey to the Rocky Mountains with Sir Sandford Fleming, surveying routes for the future transcontinental railway. He was also editor and co-author of the famous two-volume *Picturesque Canada*, published in 1882. A charter member and later president of the Royal Society of Canada, he was elected moderator of the Presbyterian Church in Canada in 1889.

# *The Implacable Educator*

*by* ROBERTSON DAVIES

When George Monro Grant left the University of Glasgow to return to his native Nova Scotia the correspondent of a London paper wrote, "Grant is a splendid fellow, the realized ideal of Kingsley's muscular Christian." In a speech at a farewell party Grant declared that his motto in college had been "What thy hand findeth to do, do it with all thy might," and added that this would also be his rallying cry in the battle of life. Thus his character was formed at the age of twenty-five, and deepened, but did not alter, until his death at sixty-seven.

The sense of destiny was strong in Grant. His mother could not conceal her preference for this third of her five children, and asserted that "God had a purpose for him." Here was mighty magic in a family where it was accepted that "Mother can't be wrong." Nor was his father far behind in encouragement; he was wont to say, "George will do what is right." Fortified by religion and parental love, how could Grant fail?

He failed but once, and that was in an early attempt to establish a theological hall at Dalhousie. Through sixteen years as a minister (fourteen of them in a Halifax pulpit which he made influential), through adventures as a traveller with Sandford Fleming's two expeditions across the continent, through twenty-five years in which he raised Queen's University from sore straits to a well-founded institution with an admirable faculty and an endowment, he never failed in any other serious venture.

For those who do not warm to a tale of unbroken success it may be added that Grant had his misfortunes, personal and domestic. When he was seven he lost his right hand playing with a haycutter; his second son would now be called a retarded child, who died, deeply mourned, when he was twelve; Grant's beloved wife, Jessie Lawson, was an invalid for nearly thirty years, and it is part of the measure of their love that he did

not long survive her. But of public failure there was no hint; Grant was a man of many causes, and when he undertook one of his public tasks he was striving not for himself but for the public good; in that he could conceive of nothing so manifestly contrary to the Divine Will as failure.

His son writes of him as speaking "with the calm self-confidence of one who felt himself to be a steward of the oracles of God." Such men may be admired, and he was; they are often loved, and he was; but they are also feared. An amateur of horoscopes will notice that Grant was born under Capricorn, the determined striver, and was strongly under the influence of Saturn, that chill and minatory planet. A man who was a Queen's student when Grant was in his heyday recalls a student song:

*Does you know the famous George Monro, the leader of the band?*
*Does you? We does!*
*Does you think there ain't his equal in this or any land?*
*Does you? We does!*

But the tone changes at the end of the verse–

*Does you always run to meet him when you see that pleasant smile?*
*Now does you? Why NO!*

It was Grant's custom to smile broadly when trouble was brewing–a characteristic inherited by his son. A man whose smile is a dreadful omen is at least as much a child of Saturn as of the Presbyterian Church.

Grant was a famous and deadly controversialist whose devotion to principle was a source of amusement to his friend, Sir John A. Macdonald. Visiting Kingston before a general election, Sir John dined one night at his sister's table, with Grant as the other guest; as soon as the meal was over Macdonald excused himself by saying that he had business in the town, and left his flustered sister and the somewhat affronted Principal of Queen's to make what conversation they might. When Macdonald's sister asked him later where he had gone, he said, "Oh, I wanted to talk with the Negro barber. It's no use glaring at me; the barber controls six votes, and now I control the barber. But Grant–you know he'll always vote according to his conscience."

It was to Grant that Macdonald made his famous rejoinder when the Principal assured him that he would always support him when he was in the right. "My dear fellow," said Macdonald, "what I need is men who'll support me when I'm in the wrong."

Any suggestion that Grant delighted in the legend of his own greatness would be unjust. His character was as simple in essence as his life was complex in deed. He liked the sweets of life–especially "well-appointed dinners"–but would not justify them as a personal indulgence. He loved society, was renowned for his vivacity, and had a strong measure of Highland gallantry that made him popular with women. His literary style is characteristic–impatient, vivid, unadorned and, it must be said, unselective and unimaginative. There is no hint of the artist here.

It was as a university administrator that he was greatest. He built up the fortunes of Queen's by stumping the country, begging. His harvest was not in thousands and millions, but in five and ten-dollar bills. Nay, he would not have despised a single dollar from a well-wisher who had no more. He gave half his own stipend as principal back to the university and if he ground the faces of his staff–and he did–it was for Queen's. A principal who wore a plaid instead of an overcoat did not have to apologize for demanding sacrifice from others.

His favourite joke was that his epitaph would surely be from the sixteenth chapter of Luke: "And it came to pass that the beggar died." He knew perfectly that the verse continues, "and was carried by the angels into Abraham's bosom." Queen's has never doubted that that was what happened to the principal.

# Harold Adams Innis

1894-1952

A monumental political economist and historian, recognized as the leading social scientist in Canada, he had, at the time of his death, "an international reputation equalled by that of no other Canadian scholar." Born at Otterville, Ontario, educated at McMaster, Toronto and Chicago universities, he produced nine volumes of history in his comparatively short life and edited many others. During this period he rose from lecturer in political science at the University of Toronto (1920) to head of the department in 1937 and dean of the School of Graduate Studies (1947). His approach to history broke fresh ground and led to a new understanding of the forces behind Canadian nationhood.

# *The Stubborn Scholar*

by DONALD CREIGHTON

The University of Toronto has named the newest of its new colleges Innis College, in memory of one of its own scholars. The honour is unusual, perhaps unprecedented. But Innis more than deserved it. If any one man can stand for the university tradition in Canada, it is Harold Innis. He believed in the university as one of the main buttresses of Western civilization. He not only worked in a university; he lived in it. He thought, worried, talked and gossiped about it with inexhaustible interest. He was rigidly unbending in upholding its highest standards. He stubbornly defended what he believed to be its rights and privileges. The academic world of Canada, and much of the same world in England and the United States, was as well known to him as if it had been a small village in which he had grown up. He knew the politics and personalities of every institution of higher learning in this country. He relished and related academic gossip and good stories with infectious gusto. A tall, slight man with a thin face, a mobile mouth, and a long, unruly lock of hair, he would sit, usually in a straight, hard chair, tilting it slightly backward, and talk for hours of the world of scholarship and of the ideas, books and men that made it up.

Innis was an economist with a special interest in Canadian economic history; but few Canadian historians have been less limited by the boundaries of their country. Innis's work ranged far outward in space and backward in time. *The Fur Trade in Canada* became a study of continental rivalries in North America. *The Cod Fisheries* broadened into a vast chronicle of the rise and fall of empires on the North Atlantic. His final work, which began as an investigation into the Canadian pulp and paper industry, gradually took on the huge proportions of a treatise on communications through the ages and stretched backward in time to Babylonian cuneiform tablets and Egyptian papyrus. At these huge enterprises Innis worked with unflagging zeal and tireless industry. Yet his own work was never a mere laborious accumulation of material. He interpreted his vast masses of evidence imaginatively, at times intuitively; and his insight carried him to remote and unexpected conclusions which a more pedestrian scholar would never have reached. His books were strong with facts, but lively with daring hypotheses and sweeping generalizations.

He was the helpful, loyal friend of many people, and the genial, entertaining companion of many more; but when a question of intellectual values or academic standards was at stake, he could become a difficult, stubborn, and obstructive man. If the issue were serious enough, he was prepared to use the ultimate available form of protest. He didn't hint at resignation, or threaten resignation. He simply resigned. When the Royal Society of Canada awarded one of its medals to the author of a literary work which Innis considered unworthy of the prize, he temporarily gave up his fellowship in the society in order to force a revision of the regulations governing the award. Twice at least he resigned from the University of Toronto, once when he was quite young and once–as his horrified friends doubtless considered–when he was certainly old enough to know better. On the latter occasion he was persuaded in the end to give up his extreme stand; but often he gained his point through his quiet, inflexible determination.

He fought to preserve the highest standards in the university. He fought equally hard to defend the university in the community and the state. For him, the university tradition, the tradition of scholarship, free and critical inquiry, was the essence of Western civilization. He believed that the state must regard the preservation of this tradition as a basic responsibility, and that the members of the university community must maintain and uphold it at all times, in war as well as in peace. The best contribution scholars could make to winning the war, he always insisted, was to stick to their posts in the universities, to continue their teaching, and to keep up their scholarly inquiries.

Only by discovering, encouraging, and training its best brains could a democracy survive and grow. This training of the "most active and energetic minds" must go on in war as it did in peace; it must go on, he firmly believed, in all branches of learning, whether they made an immediate contribution to the war, as in science and medicine, or whether, as in the humanities and the social sciences, they did not. In 1942, when a change in Canada's manpower regulations threatened to leave the few remaining students in the liberal arts liable to conscription, Innis flung himself wholeheartedly into the defense of the young scholars in these venerable academic disciplines. "The arts tradition and particularly the strength of the social sciences," he wrote in a memorandum to the prime minister, "is the touchstone of democracy."

He believed in the defense of Western civilization and of the spirit of free inquiry which, for him, was its most vital element; but he never subscribed to the popular postwar conviction that "the West" was and ought to remain an ideological power bloc in necessary and inevitable opposition to the Communist world. A convinced individualist, with a strong belief in the value of human personality and the need of intellectual freedom, he was sceptical and critical of the power of the national state; he showed an equally strong dislike of the authority of the new super-powers which now began to command the allegiance of a group of satellite followers on both sides of the Cold War. For him this was imperialism, however it chose to call itself; and imperialism, in whatever allegedly good cause it asserted its crude power, was suspect and dangerous. The United States, he was convinced, was an inexperienced and therefore aggressive and blundering imperialist leader; he came to believe that Canada could best protect its own separate identity and at the same time help to preserve the peace of the world by adopting an attitude of critical detachment from the United States and by associating itself with the forces in England and Europe that were attempting to restrain the extravagances of American leadership. He was sceptical of Canada's ability to withstand the heavy weight of American commercialism and propaganda; he doubted seriously whether the politicians at Ottawa had enough independence of spirit to attempt serious resistance.

"I found Ottawa, especially the department of external affairs, very fatiguing–in fact exhausting . . ." he wrote to a correspondent in England, after an extended visit to the capital. "There is very little intellectual atmosphere around the place, and one feels how much we have lost to the United States. We follow along and kid ourselves we are our own masters."

At a dinner given in November, 1964, to mark the opening of Innis College, Vincent Bladen, an old friend and former colleague of Harold Innis who had become dean of arts and science at the University of Toronto, spoke to a large company about the "Innis tradition." The Innis tradition, a tradition at once austere and daring, is more than a body of teaching for the guidance of undergraduates in their studies; it is also a set of distinctive and lofty standards and a critical and independent outlook on public affairs. It is to be hoped that the Innis tradition will be honoured not merely in words but also in deeds.

# Stephen Butler Leacock

1869-1944

The best-known humorist in the English-speaking world, he was also a serious and respected political economist. Born in Swanmore, Hampshire, England, he was educated at Upper Canada College, where he later became a master, and at the University of Toronto. He joined the political science department of McGill in 1903, became its head in 1908, and held that position until his retirement in 1936. A pioneer political economist, he was the author of more than sixty books including such serious works as *Elements of Political Science*. But it is for *Nonsense Novels, Literary Lapses, Sunshine Sketches of a Little Town* and more than thirty other works of humour translated into languages that include Gujarati and Japanese that he will be best remembered.

# The Humorist

by ERIC NICOL

Stephen Leacock did an amazing thing. He proved to the world that Canadians were capable of laughter.

Before his time attempts had been made to show that there was no fundamental incompatibility between laughter and the character of the Canadian people, but the world remained unconvinced. All the foreigner could go by was the demeanour of the Canadians he met, either in their own country or abroad, and from this experience he judged that the gamut of Canadian expression ranged from glum to downright dour.

The world knew that the Canadian soldier was brave and resourceful, the Canadian politician bland and non-toxic, Canadian womanhood wholesome, Canadian bacon lean. But despite the efforts of natives like Haliburton, Canadians' having a sense of humour remained a hypothesis, considerably less substantiated than the ability of the natives of Mbengga to walk on fire.

Then came Leacock. A Canadian. Writing funny books. An achievement comparable to the journey of the little RCMP ship *St. Roch* breaking through the arctic ice to become the first vessel to circumnavigate North America. Leacock discovered the Northwest Passage to world recognition of Canada as a country where humour was not necessarily locked in eternal freeze-up.

As his funny pieces appeared year after year in American periodicals like *Vanity Fair* and the old *Life*, the United States hailed his comic genius. This was the major factor in convincing Canadians that Leacock was in fact a great humorist. Without the reassurance from south of the line Canadians would have chuckled at Leacock, perhaps, and admitted that he was quite a wag living up Orillia way with that crazy family of his–"Mama Leacock was the funniest of the lot, they say"–but it would not have occurred to us to mention him in the same breath with Benchley or Thurber or Wodehouse.

Even today, among Canada's professional aesthetes, of which the supply considerably exceeds the demand, there is chagrin that Leacock is not only an internationally admired representative of Canadian letters but also *the* representative. Open any contemporary U.S. anthology of twentieth-century literature, and the prohibitive odds are that a Leacock essay is the sole bit of Canadiana to make the grade. To the high priests of pomposity that charge themselves with examining the entrails of the arts in Canada, it is distressing to find this same rude pebble–a humorist–crowding the craw.

Leacock just does not fit into auguries uttered for the benefit of ballet, drama, symphonic music–all those fine arts that qualify as serious by the

unmistakable and invariable fact that they lose money. Leacock made money. Pots of it. People bought his books and flocked to his lectures (the ones he gave outside McGill). Thus he bears a double brand of shame: he was a funnyman, and he made it pay outrageously. If he had written something in the true-bluer vein of today's anti-comedy, or if he had lived long enough to apply for a Canada Council grant on the ground of impecuniosity, Canada's literary historians might have found it in their hearts to forgive him. But Leacock was that most suspect of all Canadian types, a success. He dared to rise above the vast mediocrity of his literary compatriots, and that he did it just for fun, or was otherwise impaired at the time, is no mitigating factor. If somebody were to paint a tableau of the Fathers of Canadian Culture, Leacock would be the farthest below the salt.

What unsettles the custodians of Canada's arts more than anything else, however, is that Leacock's humour takes a strip off twaddle. And twaddle is the mothballing with which we in this country preserve our cultural identity.

Leacock joyfully satirized the literary vogues of his time, and our *litterateurs* chafe under the burry fact that no Canadian literary hero has become as memorable as the stalwart of "Gertrude the Governess" who "flung himself from the room, flung himself upon his horse and rode madly off in all directions." Here is the hero with whom all Canadians can identify: the ass on the horse, the Mountie transcendental, getting his man, or woman, by sheer fragmentation of all points of the compass.

Leacock the professor threw the dry chalk of his wit at education's follies. The follies have survived, got fatter, but today's educators, clinging to the ballooning system of mass lecturing, cannot but wince at the rasping irony with which he defined higher education (*Oxford As I See It*) as a highly personal relationship—"what an Oxford tutor does is to get a little group of students together and smoke at them. Men who have been systematically smoked at for four years turn into ripe scholars."

With the desperation born of humbug, Canadian educators, politicians and like pillars of society have stressed that Leacock was first of all a professor of economics, author of solid tomes on the subject, and was only incidentally a humorist. The good, grey flock of domestic fowl point at the webbed foot as proof that this high-flying whooper was also a goose.

Yet remorselessly the publishers continue to reprint the humorous Leacock. New generations of Canadians sense with glee the symbolic truth of the Sunshine Sketches, recognize that Canada's ship of state, never destined to test the turbulent deep of history's oceans, sinks as the *Mariposa Belle* settled gently, and perennially, into the reedy shallows of Lake Wissanotti.

The operative word is "Sunshine." The light that Leacock casts on our foolishness is warm. We sometimes forget that the sun too is a nuclear explosion, a fission of angry forces. Leacock was angry, furious at stupidity, materialism, hypocrisy, sham—the whole twentieth-century panoply of utter rot. But his reaction was the controlled and benign explosion of laughter.

Like the sunshine, we take it for granted, this very complicated process of dispelling darkness pleasantly. Our later era of "sick" humour attacks the dark with a harsh fluorescence that is not nearly as kind to the shadows under our eyes.

Will Leacock last? The answer to that ponderous question must be: no, Leacock will not last, will start to dim from that day when people no longer go into the bank to open their first savings account; when club chairmen introduce the guest speaker without expressing regret at the "poor turnout tonight;" when people read the classics without regard to intellectual snobbery; when economics is a science as pellucid as a glass of grain alcohol; when boarding-house geometry discards the datum that a landlady is "a parallelogram, that is, an oblong, angular figure, which cannot be described, but which is equal to anything."

Stephen Leacock left us laughter that may well prove as ephemeral as that other solar radiance that brightens our lives.

# Paul-Emile Cardinal Léger

1904-

French Canada's leading churchman, and a world figure as a result of his key role at Vatican congresses, was born at Valleyfield, Quebec, the son of a storekeeper, educated in Montreal and Paris and ordained in the Sulpician Order in 1929. He founded for his order a seminary at Fukuoka, Japan, where he taught philosophy from 1933 to 1939. In 1940 he was named vicar-general of the diocese of Valleyfield and in 1947 rector of the Pontifical Canadian College in Rome. He was created Archbishop of Montreal in 1950 and Cardinal in 1953. In 1963 he was made a member of the Vatican Consistorial Congress.

# *The Radical Priest*

*by* PETER GZOWSKI

One of the most fascinating questions about the role of the Roman Catholic Church in Quebec's revolution of the 1960s—and therefore one of the most fascinating questions in all Canadian history—is whether the Church has been surprised at the part played in that revolution by Canada's most eminent Catholic, Paul-Emile Cardinal Léger. By the middle 1960s, it had become abundantly clear that Léger, along with such European cardinals as Bea and Suenens and Frings, and such Americans as Ritter and Meyer, was a staunch member of the wing of the Church most easily described as liberal; that he was, indeed, one of the Church's *most* liberal princes. At the third session of the Second Vatican Council, for instance (and to choose only one small example), Léger made what one Catholic writer calls "the strongest statement of any Council Father on the question of religious freedom."

"We must affirm," Léger said, "freedom of religion for everyone, including those who have no religion at all." But in 1950, when he was appointed archbishop of Montreal, the likelihood of Paul-Emile Léger's fulfilling such a role in world Catholicism—or, for that matter, of any French-Canadian churchman's fulfilling such a role—must have seemed about as strong as the likelihood of Maurice Duplessis's becoming a Witness of Jehovah.

The secular power of the Catholic clergy in Quebec was, in 1950, nearly two full centuries old. The clergy had stepped into the vacuum left when most of French Canada's ruling classes returned to France after the Battle of the Plains of Abraham in 1759. In the years up to and including the ascendancy of *duplessisme* they had relinquished little of their control over temporal matters. Léger's predecessor as archbishop, Joseph Charbonneau (who came, not incidentally, from Ontario), had taken some steps in a "liberal" direction—he had fought for the workers in Quebec's bitter Asbestos strike of 1949—and had been summarily deposed.

At first glance, Léger must have seemed to the bishops and the politicians who had urged Charbonneau's firing to be a highly satisfactory replacement. He had been raised under the strict discipline of provincial Quebec and by the *robes-noirs* of St. Anicet and Valleyfield. His theological studies were conducted at the Grand Seminary of Montreal, and, as a brief biography published by the University of Notre Dame Press notes, "there could have been few opportunities within its silent, grey walls, cavernous corridors and classrooms

to develop the qualities the modern world demands in a priest." From his ordination until his appointment as archbishop, Léger had spent little time outside the walls of seminaries or churches—and little of that in Canada. He had spent four years studying and teaching in France; six planning and administering a seminary in Japan; three as rector of a college in the Vatican. His experience of Quebec was confined to one term as vicar-general of his home diocese, Valleyfield. While he was there, one liberal Catholic layman recalled in a much later conversation, "he seemed like poison to all the things that the young people and the progressive people were trying to do in the church." Montreal in 1950, already feeling the first turbulent currents of what was to erupt ten years later, must have seemed a foreign city to him.

If it did, it did not remain so for long. The men who expected Archbishop Léger to accept what he found in Montreal failed to understand the central fact of his character. Above all else, Léger was and is a deeply religious man, as if he were a Christian first, a Catholic second and a priest third. This is a quality that has not been common, over the years, to all the clergy of French Canada, and it is one that, we may assume, surprised some people who did not know Léger well. Exposed to the forces and pressures of Montreal, Léger began to undergo what the American authority who writes under the name Xavier Rynne calls an "interior revolution" of his own. "Though he began his career as a Sulpician, under the tutelage of the old-guard French-Canadian hierarchy," Rynne wrote in his book *Letters From Vatican City*, "Léger is now a staunch advocate of that reform of the Church that aims at getting back to the fundamental roots, and would restore Catholicism today as a mystery-conscious, apostolic-minded, yet tolerant institution, along the lines of the primitive Church."

From the outset of his prelacy in Montreal, Léger invited advice from all quarters, no matter how dissident. He listened with compassion to the views of many critics of the Church—even to such outspoken Catholics as the editors of the radical magazine *Cité Libre*, whom he heard in a private discussion in the early 1950s. The man who had been so much out of the real world for so long brought an open mind and an open heart to its realities; by the time he received his red hat, in 1953, Léger had moved a long way from being "poison" to the young liberal Catholics of only a decade before.

In many ways, Léger's approach to his role in Montreal in the early 1950s anticipated the views of the liberal Pope John XXIII. He worked to reinvigorate that most fundamental root of any church, the laity, and he took an interest, in his own archdiocese, in the beginnings of the ecumenical movement. By the time John was elected to the papacy, Léger was a central figure of Catholic ecumenicalism; he was asked to go to Rome for ten days of each month preceding the Second Vatican Council, to help lay the foundation for that giant stride forward. And during the council itself, Léger's voice was raised on the liberal side of many vital discussions of the Church's future.

But for all his eminence as a world figure, it is for his influence on French Canada that most Canadians will likely want to remember Cardinal Léger longest. He had worked to bring lay teachers and administrators—and therefore new freedom and new vigour—into every level of education. By 1962 he could point proudly to the fact that seventy percent of the teaching hours in the *collèges classiques* of his archdiocese were in the hands of the laity. He has sought to modernize both the image and the practices of the clergy under his leadership. He has surrounded himself with bright, energetic young priests and he has worked inexhaustibly himself. Because of his Christian concern for the problems he was once thought not to comprehend, he has changed the Church in Quebec almost as dramatically as Quebec itself has changed. And because of those changes the Church has made itself a vital part of the revolution in Quebec, rather than a victim of it.

# Sir William Osler

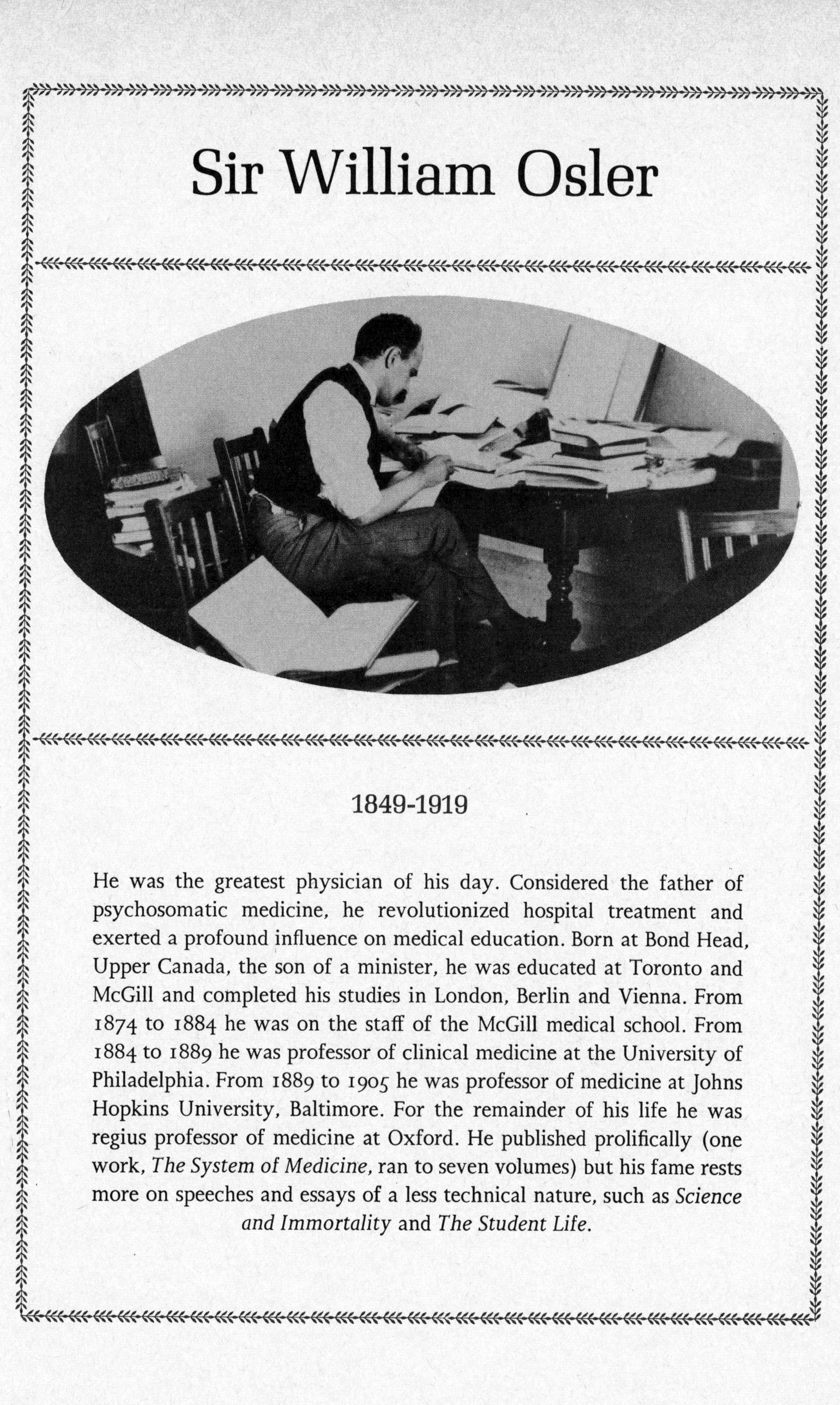

1849-1919

He was the greatest physician of his day. Considered the father of psychosomatic medicine, he revolutionized hospital treatment and exerted a profound influence on medical education. Born at Bond Head, Upper Canada, the son of a minister, he was educated at Toronto and McGill and completed his studies in London, Berlin and Vienna. From 1874 to 1884 he was on the staff of the McGill medical school. From 1884 to 1889 he was professor of clinical medicine at the University of Philadelphia. From 1889 to 1905 he was professor of medicine at Johns Hopkins University, Baltimore. For the remainder of his life he was regius professor of medicine at Oxford. He published prolifically (one work, *The System of Medicine*, ran to seven volumes) but his fame rests more on speeches and essays of a less technical nature, such as *Science and Immortality* and *The Student Life*.

# *The Gentle Healer*

*by Dr.* WILDER GRAVES PENFIELD

The most illustrious physician in Canadian history was born, as he once expressed it, "with every advantage–eighth child of an Anglican missionary in Upper Canada with twins ahead." William Osler's mother was a resourceful little woman with the olive complexion that betrays the aboriginal Celt among Cornish folk. She was a woman of independent spirit who was to live beyond her hundredth birthday and see most of her other children lead distinguished lives in and about Toronto. William's father, Featherstone Lake Osler, also came from Cornwall but he was an adventurous, grey-eyed Anglo-Saxon.

He decided that "Willie" should enter the Church, and sent him to a newly founded school in Weston, near Toronto. But his plans went astray. The warden of the school, W. A. Johnson, although himself an Anglican minister, was a low-church Canadian with a weakness for botanical excursions. Fifty years later, when Willie had become Sir William Osler, Regius Professor of Medicine at Oxford, he wrote about his schoolboy conversion in these words:

"Ten years with really able . . . teachers left me with no more real knowledge of Greek and Latin than of Chinese, and without the free use of the language as keys to great literature. Imagine the delight of a boy of an inquisitive nature to meet a man who cared nothing about words but who knew about things–who knew the stars in their courses and who could tell us their names, who delighted in the woods in springtime, and told us about the frog-spawn and the caddis worms, and who read to us in the evenings . . . who showed us with the microscope the marvels in a drop of dirty pond water, and who on Saturday excursions up the river could talk of the Trilobites and Orthoceratites and explain the formation of the earth's crust. No more dry husks for me after such a diet . . . From the study of nature to the study of man was an easy step."

Osler began his study of medicine in 1867. He started at Toronto, then moved to Montreal and finished at McGill. He then had two years abroad, in Germany and England, and while there did some original work on blood platelets. Having used the warden's microscope as a schoolboy, he found it an easy step from swamp water to human blood. His work was presented before the Royal Society and when he returned to Canada he was invited to join the McGill faculty. At the end of a year the chair of the Institutes of Medicine fell vacant unexpectedly and, at twenty-five, Osler found himself the substitute and soon the full professor. Thus he was called upon to teach what was known as physiology and microscopic anatomy.

This was a wonderful challenge to a young man with an independent, inquiring mind. At the Montreal General Hospital, he volunteered to carry out the autopsies for all the other doctors. When they agreed he became the hospital's first pathologist, a voluntary one. For ten years he had few private patients and very little money, for he was always in hospital ward, library or laboratory.

But he was gay, full of spirit, and popular among his fellows. What his first teacher, Palmer Howard, called the Osler ferment led to new societies and innovations. His personal life was adjusted to a regular rhythm of work and study, gaiety and reading. He was not a good speaker or a polished writer at the start. But, by dint of hard work, he acquired rare skill.

When at thirty-five he was called to the chair of medicine at the University of Pennsylvania, he turned to clinical medicine, critically and as one who, having studied the causes of disease, would accept no precept without proof. During his five years in Philadelphia he assembled evidence for, and began writing, a textbook of medicine that was based on the scientific method, presented in polished prose and seasoned with humour.

In 1898 he moved to Baltimore to become the first professor of medicine in the recently founded and already famous Johns Hopkins University and Hospital. He did return to Philadelphia, briefly, when he married Grace Revere Gross, widow of his former colleague, the surgeon Samuel Gross.

During his sixteen years in Baltimore he introduced the method of teaching medicine at the bedside as he had learned it in the Montreal General Hospital, adding German laboratory methods. Still more important, he led in the movement to sweep away traditional treatment, relying instead only on the evidence to be found in the study of nature and disease. He was criticized and called a therapeutic nihilist. But the avalanche of medical discoveries had begun, discoveries of the specific causes of specific diseases. There was need of a leader who would forbid useless treatment, who would make way for modernization. Osler was that leader, a sort of John the Baptist in a wilderness of medical superstition.

He retired from Johns Hopkins at fifty-six and sailed away to Oxford with his wife and his only son, Revere Osler. There he devoted himself less to medicine and more to literature and medical bibliography. He took delight in book collecting and made scholarly addresses that had to do with a physician's way of life rather than with science. Several volumes of such essays were published. They outran his textbooks in popularity.

It was at Oxford during Osler's tenure that I carried out my first post-mortem examination. I screwed my courage to the sticking place and had made a beginning when I was startled by the voice of Sir William. He had entered the room unobserved. "That is splendid," he said. "It is always best to do a difficult job the wrong way first. Then you never forget."

His coat was off and he was pulling on a pair of autopsy gloves. He proceeded to demonstrate the correct technique. But he did much more that morning. He asked to be told about the departed and his loved ones. He spoke of life and death with reverence. We saw how the knowledge drawn from this defeat might teach each of us to save life when at a future bedside we encountered the condition that had brought death to this body. Or, if not to save life, at least to comfort with greater understanding. Necropsy, in Osler's hands, became for us the crowning act of a physician's compassion. Pathology was knowledge for a doctor to use. Osler liked to quote the words of Froude: "The knowledge that a man can use . . . has life and growth in it . . . The rest hangs like dust about the brain or dries like raindrops off the stones."

He died in 1919 at seventy. An American disciple, Fielding Garrison, wrote: "What Osler meant to the medical profession in America, what he did for us, can never be adequately expressed . . . He was handsome, wise, witty, learned, courteous, fair-minded and brave . . . a bond between English-speaking physicians everywhere."

What is new in science today may be out of date tomorrow. But the art of medicine has in it eternal truth. It deals with the spirit of man and is forever renewed by the goodness that wells up in the nature of mankind. William Osler added something new to the physician's practice of the ancient art.

# E. J. "Ned" Pratt

## 1883-1964

He was the nearest thing to a poet laureate the country has yet produced. Born in Western Bay, Newfoundland (his father was a clergyman, his maternal grandfather a sea-captain), he began his academic career as a psychologist but in 1919 found a more permanent niche as a lecturer in English at Victoria College, University of Toronto. He became a full professor (with nine honorary degrees to his name) and remained at the college until he was named professor emeritus in 1951. Author of seventeen books of epic verse (including *Brébeuf and His Brethren* and *Towards the Last Spike*), he was awarded the Canada Council Medal in 1961-62.

Newfoundland Sailors

This is their culture, this their master passion—
Of giving shelter and of sharing bread,
Of answering rocket signals in the fashion
Of losing life to save it. In that spread
Of time— the Gilbert [illegible] Bartlett span—
The headlines cannot [illegible]
Nor calls like Lo[illegible]!
Outplay the drama[illegible]

×

The wonders fad[illegible]
Planes bank [illegible]
The caravans m[illegible] the jets
Scarce noticed [illegible]
Bracing their [illegible]
Centuries before [illegible]
That small ance[illegible]
Red-boned their [illegible] gunwales.

×

As old as i[illegible]
Enduri[illegible]
Th[illegible] the [illegible]
Of uncontract[illegible] else
On sea or la[illegible]
That without ten[illegible] commands,
A rescue squad [illegible] he lay
With the storm [illegible] hands?

E. J. Pratt

# *The Dragonslayer*

by JAMES REANEY

Malignant Cove, Ireland's Blight, Hooping Harbour, Harbour Deep, Little Harbour Deep, Jackson's Arm, Sop's Arm, Coachman's Cove, Pumbly Cove, Wild Cove, Joe Batt's Arm, Cow Head, Little Heart's Ease—these are the place names you find if you run your finger round the island Ned Pratt came from, the island of Newfoundland. It is no wonder that he grew up to be a poet and a story-teller. Newfoundland's very geography is already a poem and a story.

"The Shark," "The History of John Jones," "The Submarine," *The Witches Brew*, *The Cachalot*, *The Great Feud*, *The Roosevelt and the Antinoe*, *The Titanic*, *Towards the Last Spike*—these are some of the titles you find if you run your finger down the index to Pratt's *Collected Poems*, a volume that is fast becoming a household book in our country. The very titles of Pratt's poems suggest his interest in stories about human heroism and ships, storms, monsters—whether steam engines or muskeg bogs that swallow newly built railways—ships, storms, monsters and human heroism. This interest, coupled with a wild sense of humour and an ability to make his poems sound like talk at a party, all this story-telling ability comes out of his Newfoundland heritage. His poems are a sort of Newfoundland, a very welcome addition to the less witty, less narrative remainder of Canada.

Ned Pratt himself was a very welcome addition to the Toronto scene. His love of telling stories, jokes and of giving parties—all this enlivened the austerities of central Canada. I do not know why it is but those who teach Chaucer and Shakespeare generally do not behave like their subjects. At least we do not expect them to be Mermaid Taverners or accepted frequenters of such a sophisticated court as Richard II's must have been. Pratt taught English literature at Victoria College and not only taught it, but laughed like it.

I can remember a hotel-room party he threw in Winnipeg when he was on his way across the country doing the research for *Towards the Last Spike*. In explaining to me the feeling he was trying to get about the land of Canada, the very rocks themselves—with a glass in one hand he flung out the other and said, "You know, Jimmie—all those fossils." Somewhat later, after a dinner given at his expense—a dinner that was probably the first and the last truly sumptuous meal I shall ever devour—I can remember a whole evening of talk and stories. Since Pratt is dead now, one will not have the chance to experience his laughter or generosity again. That's wrong, of course. These qualities, as well as others more hidden at the personal level, appear in his poetry, and it is around this new found land created by Pratt out of written words that I should now like the reader to sail with me.

The first thing a reader is apt to notice is that a section in Pratt's *Collected Poems* called *Titans*, containing a narrative poem about dinosaurs and also one about a whale, is dedicated "To the boys of the stag parties." Pratt's poems are not friendly to the WCTU; he is as friendly to John Barleycorn as Burns was, and the resultant verse has the wallop and verve that men's talk has, or should have, when men are convivial.

People talk about the sound of a jazz musician. What is the Pratt sound like? Here is the inside of a whale as he describes it in *The Cachalot*:

*He was more wonderful within.*
*His iron ribs and spinal joists*
*Enclosed the sepulchre of a maw.*

Obviously he loves words and long hard words as well as short fat easy ones. You can get addicted to the Pratt sound, and if you think he has given you his most outrageous rhyme, there will always pop up a new one that seems even more outrageous:

*You oldest of the hierarchs*
*Composed of electronic sparks.*

This latter is from a remarkable poem called "The Truant" in which man comically and heroically answers back to the oldest of the hierarch-tyrants – the sinister awful world of fate, of the stars, of the outer space we sometimes imagine as dwarfing us. Never make the mistake of regarding Pratt as a light poet; behind the comic-sounding lurches and revving-up noises stands the sort of laughter that dares to express itself in the face of the hostile universe we live in. This "hostile universe" usually appears in Pratt as some sort of monster, and perhaps his monsters are the next thing after his sound that we should consider.

Dragons are good to tell stories about. Pratt evidently heeded the advice that if you want to tell a good story put a dragon into it, because a great many of his story poems contain such a being or its representative. They come in many shapes – in his poem about the building of the CPR, *Towards the Last Spike*, the muskeg country north of Lake Superior is seen as a lizard – "On the North Shore a reptile lay asleep." After reading that line, perhaps you may remember the feeling that the northern Ontario landscape gives you on a train journey, the feeling of a hostile, brooding, ancient presence, far more eerie and, of course, far more ancient than the much larger-looking Rocky Mountains.

Now most people go through life with no feeling that they are facing monsters every day, perhaps only with a sensation that life can be occasionally dreary. That dreariness is what a poet with Pratt's special kind of X-ray vision diagnoses as a dragon, because boredom and meaninglessness are exactly as lethal as a fire-eating monster. Pratt makes you see this fact of our spiritual existence – the terror in the stars, the terror in the ice floes, the terror in our past when during Alexander Mackenzie's prime ministership we were afraid to continue with the railway, afraid of the huge spaces involved. In the end, Pratt implies over and over again, and this is a great idea around which we can build our lives, he implies over and over again that if we can defeat the terror within ourselves, we will find that we have defeated the monster that caused the terror.

Where does Pratt think that the ability to conquer fear comes from? He thinks that the strength comes from the special truant laughter already mentioned; in some of his poems, notably *Brébeuf and His Brethren*, the ability to conquer comes from Christ, who perhaps is the same as the special kind of laughter. The Iroquois torturers try to find the source of Brébeuf's courage by digging out his heart, but the source is really

*. . . two slabs of board, right-angled, hammered*
*By Roman nails and hung on a Jewish hill.*

It is a remarkable poet who can range from "the boys at the stag parties" to the "two slabs of board" mentioned above. All of life stands between. It is also a remarkable poet who, born at one end of a huge country, lived to write the story, his last story, the story of how we as a people managed, after thirteen years of effort, to drive in a Last Spike and so possess the other end of our country. Between his birth and his death Pratt came to know the Canada between Joe Batt's Arm and Bella Bella so well that his poetry will always be able to tell us more about ourselves than we ourselves know.

# Gabrielle Roy

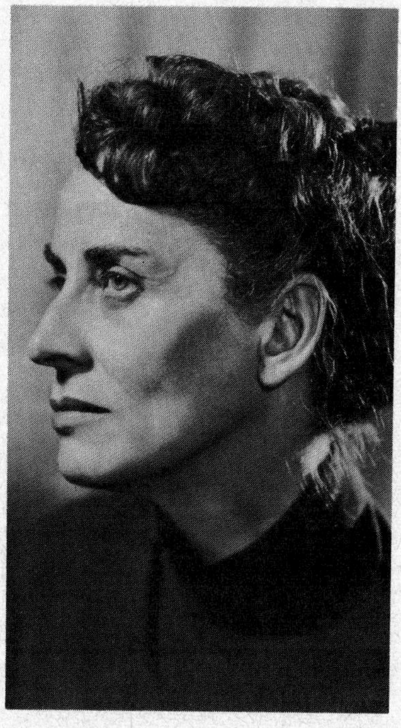

1909-

A leading novelist in both French and English Canada, she was born in St. Boniface, Manitoba. During the course of an early teaching career she became interested in the theatre, twice winning the French trophy. In 1937 she went to Paris to study drama, returning to Montreal in 1939. She began her literary career writing reportorial articles for various periodicals. In 1945, she achieved an international reputation for her story of life in an industrial district of Montreal, *Bonheur d'Occasion*, published in English as *The Tin Flute*. Three other novels followed, together with France's *Prix Fémina* and the French Academy's medal.

# The Woman on Horseback

by BRIAN MOORE

A few years ago Alfred A. Knopf, a leading American publisher, visited Canada to study the country's book trade. When he had completed his survey, a reporter asked his opinion of Canadian reading habits. "What this country needs," said Mr. Knopf, "is a Sinclair Lewis."

This answer baffled the citizenry. Sinclair Lewis, a very *American* author, won a Nobel prize for his caustic portrayal of the uncultured "hick" mentality in small midwestern U.S. towns in the 1920s and was, in his day, the scourge of the average American businessman. Why did we Canadians need a Lewis in the 1960s? Unruffled, Mr. Knopf explained. Lewis's *Main Street* was the first American novel discussed, not in literary salons, but in the corner store, in the local golf club and in homes throughout the small towns of America. It was the first novel to criticize the "average" American and, because of this, Americans read it, argued about it and condemned it. Canada, Mr. Knopf believed, has not yet had a Sinclair Lewis.

This may be true. But Canada, as we are often reminded these days, is not the United States. Sinclair (Red) Lewis, an irascible, raucous author, is a most un-Canadian figure. It seems likely that, if a Canadian Lewis appeared on the scene, he or she would be a milder, more agreeable personality. It can be argued that a Canadian Lewis has already appeared, and that she is a tiny ex-schoolmistress from Manitoba, no loud-mouthed smiter-down of the Philistine but a mild-mannered, almost prim person, whose writing, in the freestyle 1960s, seems an echo of Victorian propriety.

Yet twenty years ago this lady delivered the first verbal bomb in the Donnybrook of racial discussion which has since swept Canada from Atlantic to Pacific. It can further be said that after reading her first novel, *Bonheur d'Occasion* (*The Tin Flute*), a great many French and English Canadians never felt the same again.

*The Tin Flute* is set in Montreal at the beginning of World War II. Yet, as one turns its pages, one might have slipped back into the grinding, odoriferous poverty of Dickens's England or Emil Zola's France. But with this difference. From the very first page, Mlle. Roy's reader experiences an eerie prickle of recognition, a warning that he cannot be lulled by the sense that these things happened in far-off lands in far-off times. These horrors are contemporary. The book opens at the lunch counter in a five-and-ten-cent store. The heroine is a young French-Canadian waitress, and the hopeless apathy of her surroundings is Canadian, in a Canada many of us have forgotten, in a land cut off from America and from Europe, a land where twenty cents an hour was the going wage if you were lucky enough to get it, a land whose people lived from dollar to dollar, where men passed whole decades on relief, a country run out of steam and stranded, a country whose future seemed dim. In the working-class district of St. Henri (on the wrong side of the tracks from Westmount, Montreal's prosperous English-speaking enclave) we meet, for the first time in Canadian fiction, the rumble of a revolution not yet dreamed of, a deep discontent–felt rather than thought, a rural people sunk in urban poverty, a race without pride, without hope, without leadership.

Who was this woman, this Canadian, who wrote of French Canada from the inside, yet with a cold, dispassionate honesty which chilled her readers with the dread suspicion that this was less fiction than fact? Literary revolutions, like political ones, must wait for what revolutionists call "a man on horseback" to lead them. Miss Roy came on horseback. She was French, but had been born and educated on the prairies; she had studied drama in London and Paris, but had returned to Canada to live among the poor French of Montreal. Her novel, published in French in 1945, sailed like a fairy ship through all the reefs of ignorance and indifference on which most first novels founder and die ignored. First, there was French Canada, where the book was read with astonishment at its honesty and discussed not only in the literary salons of Montreal and Quebec, but in corner stores and in ordinary living rooms. Then France, where Miss Roy became the first Canadian to be awarded the influential *Prix Fémina*, a literary award so renowned that it could not be ignored in America and in Canada. With a blaze of publicity, the book was translated into English and unleashed as the May, 1947, selection of the huge U.S. Literary Guild, with a first printing of half a million copies. St. Henri had become a site in Canadian literary history. Things could never be the same again.

Miss Roy, perhaps without fully knowing it, had become the prophet of a future French-Canadian intellectual revolution. She was also, through her novel, one of the first voices of reason in discussing the two Canadas. There is a French saying that to understand all is to forget all. In her successful attempt to make French Canada's urban poor come alive on the printed pages, she made their ignorance, their intransigence, their lack of "patriotism" understandable, and sometimes pathetic. Her novel may seem, in parts, sentimental, even contrived. Yet its value was never simply literary. She came on horseback: she was the right writer, in the right place, at the right time. Other writers would follow her and she, herself, would go on to become the author of other commendable novels. But, as she said herself at the time of English publication of *The Tin Flute*: "A path is opening. We (French Canadians) are forgetting to be afraid of ourselves and getting away from the habit of imitating others. We are getting down to our own truth and to our own experiences."

# Sir Charles Saunders

1867-1937

The man who changed the face of the wheatfields with his development, in 1904, of the famous Marquis strain, was born in London, Ontario, and educated at Toronto and Johns Hopkins universities (where he studied singing) and at the Sorbonne. He was professor of chemistry and geology at Central University, Kentucky, between 1893 and 1895. From 1903 to 1922, when he retired, he was Dominion Cerealist at the Ottawa Experimental Farm. Following Marquis he developed other strains, Ruby, Garnet and Reward, all adapted to prairie conditions. Winner of the Royal Society's first Flavelle Medal in 1925, he was the author of one book, *Essais et Vers*. It had nothing to do with wheat. When he died the *Daily Express* of London wrote that "he contributed more to the wealth of his country than any other man."

# The Reluctant Genius

No Canadian of achievement ever hated the vehicle of his immortality more than did Sir Charles Edward Saunders, the reluctant developer of Marquis wheat. It was Charles Saunders's misfortune to be frail and gentle in a robust, hearty family; to fail at what he loved, the life of a concert musician; and to be vulnerable to bullying by his father, William Saunders, a selfish, hard-willed, happy hearted genius. These circumstances combined to make Charles Saunders exactly the right man to be nagged into greatness.

His conditioning began when he was a small child, bundled with his four brothers and a sister into a rented buggy by their father, who was then a self-educated druggist and chemist with a passion for horticulture. The earliest recollections of the Saunders offspring were rides through the countryside around London, Ontario, broken every few yards by lectures from their father on the Latin names of every plant in sight.

Eventually the redoubtable Will Saunders bought a farm and experimented with cross-breeding grapes, gooseberries and black currants, conscripting all his children as his assistants. Every small Saunders was an expert at plant breeding years before agricultural colleges began to teach the techniques.

Charles Saunders endured his education in creative farming patiently, but he belonged, mind and heart, to music. The Saunderses were an early model of family togetherness, spending their evenings in living-room recitals and even once, in 1882, renting a hall to present a concert. Charles played in a string quartet with his brothers but preferred the flute. He decided he wanted to go to Germany to study with a celebrated flutist. His father, however, thought he should go to Toronto to learn chemistry.

During the years when Charles earned degrees in chemistry at the University of Toronto and at Johns Hopkins, he vacationed at the family home. This had been moved to Ottawa, where Will Saunders was launching the country's first experimental farm. Charles

*by JUNE CALLWOOD*

and his brother Percy, also vacationing from his studies in chemistry, were promptly put to work feeding fertile male pollen cells into embryos, this time confining their labours to wheat. The Canadian west desperately needed a variety of wheat that would ripen early enough to survive fall frosts, and Will Saunders was cheerily crossing Canadian wheat with hardy species imported from Russia and India's Himalayan mountains. His dragooned sons once estimated that they bred some seven hundred strains themselves. Percy, who much preferred peonies, was despatched westward to plant the new varieties in experimental farms on the prairies.

Charles escaped, to marry a shy girl with a mezzo-soprano voice who shared his musical aspirations and urged him to stand on his own two feet. Together, they gave a concert in Toronto that was poorly received. Charles determinedly made his living teaching music at ladies' colleges and writing music columns in newspapers. They were starving, in a genteel way, when Will Saunders summoned his errant son to Ottawa to take over the languishing wheat research project. Heroically, Charles refused. A few days later, he was notified by telegram that he was the new Dominion Cerealist; his father had appointed him anyway. In despair, Charles moved to Ottawa.

"I am a docile person," he once observed, in monumental understatement. "I am always going where I am pushed."

Charles's real contribution to the history of Canada was chewing. The ten-year holdup in wheat development was due to a technical problem: wheat could not practically be milled in small lots, only by the carload, and it required years of careful harvesting before enough of any experimental strain could be gathered to test its flour and breadmaking qualities. Charles conceived of a dazzling shortcut – he popped a few grains of wheat in his mouth and chewed it.

The resultant gummy mass was approximately the colour that its flour would be; its glueyness foretold accurately what sort of bread it would make. Charles conscientiously chewed his way through more than a hundred varieties of wheat that he found growing neglected on the farm in Ottawa. Eventually he selected one that he thought was the best from a single stack labelled Markham. He thought it deserved a nobler name and flourishingly called it Marquis. Almost no one, of course, pronounced it the way he did.

It was probably the unhappiest period of his life. His father was a prodigious worker – in one year he sent out 11,406 letters, checking each one personally and often licking the stamps himself. Nonetheless, he found time to supervise Charles unmercifully; generally he was totally dissatisfied. Later Charles said that when he returned to Ottawa there were some fields with such bitter associations for him that he could not walk in them "without pain, without a sick feeling."

He fled his father's domination by cultivating Ottawa's French-speaking residents. He and his wife called their parties "soirées"; Mary Saunders sang at recitals and he led the Methodist choir. He was depressed much of the time but he dared not leave because his pension would be too meagre to support him. Finally his health broke and he was forced to retire, on twelve hundred dollars a year (which the government, following a public protest, later raised to five thousand dollars).

The couple at once went to Paris, where Charles announced deliriously that he felt like a new person. His French improved to such an extent that he indulged himself in a secret ambition and wrote a book of verse and essays in French, which critics in Quebec extolled as "courageous, so meritorious . . ." The French government decorated him and he made his will, leaving bequests to the French departments of the University of Western Ontario and the University of Toronto.

Just before he died in Toronto, he was so feeble of body that he could not play records on his gramophone any longer. His brother hired a young man to attend to this for him. Sir Charles Saunders, who developed the most valuable plant in world history, really loved music. He loved it all his life.

# Lord Strathcona

1820-1914

His financing of the Canadian Pacific Railway made the project possible. Born plain Donald Smith, in Scotland, he served the Hudson's Bay Company for thirty years as a fur trader in Labrador. He rose to be the company's resident governor, chief commissioner and principal stockholder. He presided over the ceding of its territories to Canada. From 1870 to 1880 he represented Selkirk, Manitoba, in the House of Commons as a Conservative. He broke with his party over the Pacific Scandal and from 1887 to 1896 represented Montreal West as an independent. For the remainder of his life he was Canadian High Commissioner in London. In 1880 he emerged as a key figure in the syndicate that built the railway and in 1887 he was named president of the Bank of Montreal, a post he held until 1905. He was in addition chancellor of both McGill and Aberdeen universities.

# *The Empire Builder*

*by* JAMES COLEMAN

Donald Alexander Smith, later Lord Strathcona, was equipped by intellect, foresight, energy and daring to have become an outstandingly successful man in any era of free enterprise: as it happened, the fires of his remarkable talents were burning brightest at the precise moment when Canada's economic and political courses almost seemed to invite the appearance of a prescient opportunist. Today, more than half a century after his death at the age of ninety-three, Strathcona remains something of an enigma to dispassionate Canadians who seek to appraise him. He left his monuments in the Canadian Pacific Railway and a clutch of impressive public benefactions. He left another legacy of those grey legends that are bequeathed to posterity by any man who has devoted himself ruthlessly to the acquisition of great wealth.

If Strathcona had pursued his career of financial freebooting in 1967, rather than 1877, his activities probably would have caused no great stir among the general public. A staff of public relations counsellors would have cultivated a benign public image for the old gentleman. But Canada was young, unsophisticated and meagrely populated when Strathcona seized his opportunity. A man who, in that era, calmly staked a personal empire, wrecked governments and seldom deigned to defend his actions with public explanations, was certain to be remembered with bitterness.

There is one familiar photographic record of Lord Strathcona – the famous photograph that shows an austere man preparing to drive the last spike of the Canadian Pacific Railway at Craigellachie, B.C., on November 7, 1885. He is sixty-five and, as he swings that trackman's sledge, he is executing the master stroke of his entire career of financial and political conniving. He is wearing a black stovepipe hat and a long black frock coat. His incredibly bushy white eyebrows are almost hidden beneath the brim of the hat. His normally grim mouth is framed by just the ghost of a smile, suggesting that this stern man is enjoying some secret joke. Most of Strathcona's jokes were secrets – or, at any rate, they were shared only by a small circle of trusted confidants. One of Strathcona's most admirable qualities was his ability to keep his own counsel. Another was his unwavering courage in the face of adversity.

The steel in his character was tempered by his early service with the Hudson's Bay Company. He was only seventeen when he arrived in Canada from Scotland and was ordered to a lonely outpost in Labrador by the autocratic Sir George Simpson, who rejoiced in such titles as King of the Fur Trade and Emperor of the Plains. Donald A. Smith, who was to become Canada's richest and most powerful man, was indentured at a salary of less than one hundred dollars a year.

When he was twenty-seven Smith was stricken in that silent wilderness by snow-blindness. He wrote three letters to Simpson, asking to be brought to Montreal for treatment. When his letters were ignored, he made the twelve-hundred-mile journey to Montreal and, unannounced, walked into Simpson's Lachine mansion at the dinner hour. The Lord of the Plains was shocked by this insubordination; but he gave Smith supper and then had him examined by his personal physician.

When the physician had offered the opinion, with some qualifications, that Smith wouldn't suffer permanent blindness, Sir George Simpson made his young subordinate pay dearly for his temerity. Simpson ordered Smith to leave Lachine and Montreal – within the next half-hour – for a new posting at bleak Esquimaux Bay. Hampered by recurrent illness along the route, Smith took four months to reach his Labrador stockade.

After years of such harsh existence, during which his extraordinary mind was whirring busily, it is understandable that Donald A. Smith may have lusted for the comforts of money and power when, in 1869, he became the dictator of the Hudson's Bay Company's operations in the west, with headquarters at Fort Garry. From this vantage point he foresaw clearly the great changes that would be wrought in that fertile land by the coming era of railway transportation. He was the one man with the audacity and the financial connections to grasp the future with both hands.

The foundations of Strathcona's vast fortune had been built with the savings of his fellow employees of the Hudson's Bay Company. Those factors and traders, who had little need of money in their isolated outposts, delegated him to invest their salaries. They asked only for an annual profit of three percent. Through his cousin George Stephen, a Montreal industrialist-banker who took the title Lord Mount Stephen, Strathcona had a direct line to the fountainhead of Canadian finance. Although he scrupulously paid the three percent interest to his fellow employees, his own profits on these investments were enormous. His silent purchases of Hudson's Bay stock actually gave him financial control of that ancient enterprise at a time when he was still, officially, its servant.

It should be remembered, then, that Strathcona was already a wealthy, superbly informed and acutely acquisitive man when the political scandal of Sir Hugh Allan's first Pacific Railway Syndicate tumbled John A. Macdonald's government. Strathcona, whose own political loyalties always were secondary to financial expediency, coolly fed John A. Macdonald to the wolves, and spent the next seven years quietly assembling the second, successful Canadian Pacific Syndicate.

The venture was a calculated risk in which one false step could have precipitated the financial ruin of his associates and their friends. The stakes were high and the gamblers were saved twice from disaster: once by the backing of the London banking firm of Barings and once by the government of a strangely forgiving John A. Macdonald. But Strathcona, who had shrewdly computed the odds to be in his favour in the long run, was the one member of the syndicate who never lost heart. It was he who stiffened the backs of his associates in the gloomiest crises.

His only concession to the probability of public criticism was this: Strathcona never himself assumed the presidency of the Canadian Pacific. That office went to Lord Mount Stephen, who was succeeded by Van Horne and then by Shaughnessy, the two brilliant railroading professionals who had been brought from the United States to assure the completion and then the successful operation of the road.

Strathcona was seventy-six and had consolidated the spoils of his financial triumphs when he went to Britain to spend his remaining seventeen years as Canada's high commissioner. He presided over that office with knee-breeched punctilio; the social graces of his last years were such that King Edward VII referred to him affectionately as "dear old Uncle Donald." But the well-banked fires still glowed. On a visit to the Okanagan Valley in his ninetieth year he was catapulted from a runaway carriage, breaking his wrist. Scorning the proffered services of a secretary, he insisted on writing lengthy official memoranda in longhand – but he worked alone behind a barred bedroom door, so that no mere mortal might witness his pain. The old man was still as tough as pemmican.

Viewed in his own context, Strathcona was a giant. It is quite probable that in any other era he would still have been a giant, casting his shadow over any land or any enterprise he marked for his own.

# Tom Thomson

1877-1917

The acknowledged father of the tradition-breaking school of landscape painting called The Group of Seven (formed shortly after his death), he was born at Claremont, Ontario. He had little formal education and was a self-taught painter who supported himself by working as a bush ranger in Algonquin Park, a setting that inspired most of his canvases. He never married, and finally drowned in the park under mysterious circumstances. He was virtually unknown and unheralded in his lifetime, but his exquisite oil sketches on small boards (8½″ x 10½″) occupy places today in all major Canadian collections. One recently sold at auction for $6400.

# *The Pathfinder*

by HAROLD TOWN

The police report might have read: "Tom Thomson . . . white . . . age forty . . . occupation artist . . . cause of death drowning . . . no water in lungs . . . bruise on head . . . copper wire around ankle . . . no witnesses." From this the legend grows: Suicide? An enemy in the bush? Drink? Freak accident? I have heard them all. In fact, a fellow art student of my youth pilfered his father's liquor cabinet and painted while drunk, for he foolishly thought that this was Thomson's way.

People are more interested in the noise about artists than in their art. If Tom Thomson had not existed, it seems likely that the general craving for a man clothed so impeccably in the basic ingredients of romance would have brought into being: a Canadian Davy Crockett art figure, completely mythological and therefore large enough to fill the great spaces of an empty land.

Even now, nearly fifty years after his death, we as a people know less of Thomson than we do of Emily Carr, who died twenty-eight-years later leaving a vast personal record of her life. Thomson's tragic death in Canoe Lake is still a mystery. The few blurred snapshots of him are like the shadow on an X-ray. Women, comprising as they do an indispensable part of the *La Bohème* tradition, are uncatalogued in his legend; yet they were there, and the perfume traces are tantalizing. He is seen often through a screen of hardship and neglect, when in fact he was supported by a kindly doctor. In 1913, at the very beginning of his personal style as a painter, his work was bought by the Ontario government, and a year later by the National Gallery of Canada. He could sleep soundly in his canoe as it bobbed in the moon's reflection, live alone in the bush for long periods, and is quoted as having said: "Take everything as it comes; the wave passes, deal with the next one." Yet he was ingenuous enough to cash a large cheque in one-dollar bills, throw them in the air and dance wildly in the descending money.

A Canadian type. With these words we touch the breathing centre of the Thomson legend: he fulfilled the need of immigrants to the new world to find an authentic, natural, native son. A loner, the quiet man, reserved, assured, stingy with talk, generous with anything else, flashing moments of wit more impressive by the rarity of its appearance. Tall, slim, dark, clean-cut, silent; all ingredients to be found in the basic handbook of character and style for pioneer, western, American man.

To most Canadians he personifies the very essence of the Group of Seven, yet he died before it was formed. As a creative entity he smouldered for most of his life (just as some of his campfires must have done in the rain). In the five years before his tragic death, he burst suddenly into flame, heating fellow artists with his compulsion for the north, and being fuelled in turn by the skill of Jackson and Macdonald, who led him to the challenge of larger pictures and the higher warmth

generated in the struggle to rid Canadian art of cookie-tin painting. Thomson seems unwittingly to have been a natural counterweight to the enervating effect of the Art Nouveau movement, brought from Europe to Canada by way of Sweden, which influenced much of the Group of Seven's formal direction and was a major factor in commercial art, by which many of the Group made a living. Thomson's skill as a commercial designer was respectable but pedestrian. Diametrically opposed to the essential failure in this effete trade, his skill in the bush was awarded the ultimate accolade of "Indian," and was professional enough to get him work as guide and fire ranger. This ability was Thomson's very personal and physical poetry; in contrast, his letters are as monumentally dull as those of a boy writing under duress to his parents from summer camp.

Thomson's small oil sketches of the last years palpitate and throb. They are as direct in attack as a punch in the nose, and the sense of movement in them has the sweep and pull of a paddle entering water. Paint is thrust and smashed onto the board with axe-like swings; it seems almost a substitute for the coarse fare of the bush, making of the final picture a banquet for Thomson's Spartan senses. "To him his most beautiful sketches were only paint," to quote his benefactor, Dr. MacCallum. It would not surprise me to find that Thomson had eaten some paint in sheer love of its completeness and tactile affinity to the tumult of colour around him in the bush.

Here then is a sense of the full creative man, yet in his painting, *A Northern Lake, 1913*, the precursor in subject matter of most later Group of Seven paintings, he points to the path taken by some contemporary, communicating landscape artists. Many of Thomson's later works antedate Borduas in slash of knife and the emotional directness of paint application. His future development seemed to lead irrevocably to abstract expressionism; in this bent, he differs completely from the painters of the Group. In spite of his desire to be true to nature, his instinctive involvement was with the act of painting, not its philosophy. His work is for the eye alone. His design, naturally sound, lost force only when touched by the influence of Art Nouveau. He failed to bring a consistent impact to his larger compositions; the studio stifled him, the big picture frightened him. It seems as though the man who lived so often by what he carried on his back lost faith in a format that could not fit his sketch box. His natural arena was a board eight by ten inches; small, yes, but truly his, and as portable as love or memories. I feel he needed nature whistling about his ears, burning his skin, soaking his shirt, before he could genuinely perform. Just as an actor wants applause, he craved the rustling quiet of that superb and (then, at least) silent land to the north. It made his hand work with final precision and felicity; he was simply a natural sketcher.

Where will Thomson stand when the final history of Canadian art is written? Unquestionably, he was mainly responsible for taking that hardy band of painters called the Group of Seven into the wilderness; and though he hadn't a quarter of the instinctive skill of Jackson or Varley, there is in his work an irrevocable quality—a joy, a solemn gaiety, a sense of youth—that makes him the natural symbol of his time.

It was a time that gave Canada its first national school of painting, and a cohesive look at the grandeur of the specific geography separating us from the rest of the continent. Thomson says: this is how it appears, there are no jokes, no satirical references, no ponderous aesthetic apparatus, no worried looks over the shoulder; the only prop is nature, and if you hear a sound, it is your heart.

In the future, as the horror of urban sprawl pollutes our past, the simplicity and honesty of his painting will not merely induce the ache of pure nostalgia, but make us long for those tender days when the fanatical love of one's own country could revolutionize national taste, and triumph over an essentially colonial establishment firmly rooted in the worst of European traditions.

Thomson was not a great painter, but he was an artist, and this is rare enough to justify his legend.

# Joseph Burr Tyrrell

1858-1957

He was the greatest land explorer of his day. Born in Weston, near Toronto, and educated at the University of Toronto, he joined the Geological Survey of Canada in 1881. After his resignation in 1898 he became a consulting geologist and mining engineer. In 1924 he was made president of the Kirkland Lake Gold Mining Co., a post he held actively until his retirement in 1954. In 1911 he edited, for the Champlain Society, Samuel Hearne's journal of his trip to Coppermine, and followed this with a similar work on David Thompson. He headed the Champlain Society from 1927 to 1932.

# *The Survivor*

*by* PIERRE BERTON

When I met him, in 1954, he was ninety-four years old and he still had three years of life left in him. In spite of his age the impression he left was one of robustness. He was a burly man, pink-cheeked and smiling, and even in those declining years he seemed to radiate health. He was the president of the Kirkland Lake Gold Mining Co. Ltd. and he was working at it.

I had come to talk to him about the Klondike stampede, for of course he had been there, in the very thick of things. He had, it seemed, been almost everywhere on the frontier in his long and fruitful career. He was old enough to be what the newspapers call "a living legend," which means he was half-forgotten. But no one could wholly forget J. B. Tyrrell. Few Canadians have left their stamp so indelibly on the land.

This was the man who, in the space of three quite incredible days in June of 1883, discovered first the dinosaur skeletons in Alberta's Red Deer Valley, and secondly a seam of bituminous coal on the present site of Drumheller. The first discovery was the single most important find of its kind on the continent; those priceless old bones grace the major museums of our time. The second discovery unearthed the largest coal deposit in Canada.

This was also the man who in 1893 and again in 1894 made with his brother two of the most remarkable land journeys in our history. Both took him across the Barren Ground – bleak, untrammelled country that had not known a white man's moccasins since the days of Samuel Hearne. In one season Tyrrell covered thirty-two hundred miles by canoe, foot and snowshoe, mapping it all with meticulous care and naming scores of lakes and rivers after everybody he knew save himself. By the time he had finished, the public's attention was riveted on the north and Tyrrell was its greatest living authority.

When I saw him he looked like a living testimonial to the lost art of walking. By all medical reasoning he ought to have been dead years before but Tyrrell, thanks to a career spent in the outdoors, had as many lives as a cat. As a youth he had suffered so badly from lung trouble that his doctor recommended a life in the woods. Tyrrell was a woodsman anyway. As a boy he had hiked the length of Toronto's Humber River, collecting almost

everything in sight: bugs, crayfish, mud turtles. The Tyrrell bathtub was a-splash with pet crayfish and the Tyrrell barn alive with rabbits and white mice. He made himself a crack shot with revolver and shotgun. He could blow out a candle with a bullet at twenty paces and knock the head off a bottle at forty.

And so, on doctor's orders, he joined the Geological Survey of Canada and set off for the Rockies to discover coal and old bones under the tutelage of that eccentric but brilliant martinet, Dr. George M. Dawson, the hunchbacked scientist who was to give his name to the country's gaudiest gold camp.

Tyrrell's subsequent achievements were all brilliant but his capacity for survival was perhaps the most brilliant of all. There was that week in the fall of 1893, out on the barrens, when he was inches from death from cold, starvation and fatigue. At the last moment the party managed to kill a polar bear. They were all so hungry they ate it right down to the entrails and the stomach's contents. The nearest pinprick of civilization, Churchill, Manitoba, was three hundred miles away and it took them another month to reach it. Tyrrell could scarcely walk, some of his companions could scarcely crawl. But when they reached Churchill he cheerily remarked that the worst was over and after a few recuperative days set off on snowshoes for Winnipeg, another nine hundred miles distant.

In his letters home there was no hint of privation. He told his wife that he dreamed every night of her pattypan cakes but when she asked if he had really gone hungry he replied, airily, that he had never missed a meal in his life though he was sometimes two or three days late for one.

Another time he found himself in the northern Manitoba wilderness, stricken with typhoid. His comrades strapped him to a stretcher of pine boughs and paddled fifteen days to Winnipeg. He recovered and named a river after the Hudson's Bay Company factor who nursed him.

In 1928, his biographer tells us, he was on the point of death: hospitalized and totally incapacitated. Again he survived but, in 1934, he was told his walking days were over forever, owing to arthritis and heart trouble. Four years later, at seventy-eight, he joined the goldrush to Yellowknife. Sixteen years after that he told a reporter that he had walked a mile the day before.

In the intervening years he continued to dazzle his colleagues.

He had been the first man to work out scientifically the reason for the presence of large deposits of placer gold in certain creeks of the Klondike. Then, at the century's turn, he quit the government service to become a private consulting engineer and publish the Dawson *Sun* on the side. He said he wanted to find out if he was worth more than eighteen hundred dollars a year.

It turned out he was. They made him president of Kirkland Lake Mining and with good reason. The company had spent a million dollars without any yield. But Tyrrell had a kind of nose for minerals. Twenty years before he had been the first to report on the great northern mineral belt which later produced Flin Flon. At Kirkland Lake he financed a deeper probe and found what he was looking for. The mine eventually yielded twenty-eight million dollars in ore. Tyrrell tried to get a group of financiers interested in another mine but was turned down. This was Teck-Hughes, which went on to produce over one hundred millions.

Among scientists he will be remembered less for these get-rich-quick achievements than as the Canadian whom the Geological Society of London ranked with Darwin, Huxley and Agassiz when it awarded him its rare *Wollaston* medal.

Among scholars he will be known for an even more lasting achievement. It was Tyrrell who singlehandedly resurrected David Thompson from the graveyard of history and put him back in the texts as the greatest of all Canadian land geographers.

When I saw him for the first and last time he was still visiting his office every day. He finally did retire, but he clung to life with the zest of one who relishes every morsel. "It's a man's duty to live as long as he can," he once declared. In this as in everything else, Joseph Burr Tyrrell achieved his goal.

# Sir William Cornelius Van Horne

1843-1915

The railroading genius who built the Canadian Pacific Railway in record time was born in Illinois in the United States and began his career in 1857 as a telegraph operator for the Illinois Central Railroad. He worked for various American railways until 1882 when, on the advice of the Great Northern's Canadian-born president, James J. Hill, the Canadian Pacific syndicate hired him as general manager to push the work of construction to completion. He was elected vice-president of the company in 1884 and president in 1888. In 1899 he became chairman of the board of directors, a post he held until he gave up his active connection with the company in 1910.

# *The Brass Pounder*

*by* TOMMY TWEED

His ambition was the highest: association with the greatest railway project ever undertaken anywhere in the world. He achieved it.

His orders were the simplest: "If you want anything done, name the day when it must be finished! If I order a thing done in a specified time and the man to whom I give that order says it is impossible to carry it out, then he must go!" He never changed them.

His personal creed was most astonishing: "I eat all I can, I drink all I can, I smoke all I can and I don't give a damn for anything." He lived by it.

William Cornelius Van Horne had learned railroading in the United States. By 1881 he had gone from telegraph messenger to acting general manager of the Chicago, Milwaukee and St. Paul Railroad. This chunky, ambitious, bearded "old timer" was thirty-eight and running on a clear track when he startled his patient wife by throwing away his future in favour of a new job at some outlandish place called Winnipeg.

It was forty below and New Year's Eve, 1881, when the new general manager of the Canadian Pacific Railway swung easily to the platform from the Milwaukee train. The weather was only slightly less chilly than the reception accorded him by local editors. "Americans," wrote one, taking patriotic umbrage, "have never been popular here in the Red River Settlement. We believe that the United States means to grab our North-west Territories just as they grabbed Oregon in 1846! As loyal, British North Americans, we have built our own railroad thus far. The Company is wrong to hire a damned, Yankee alien, and Sir John A. Macdonald is wrong to allow it!"

This stopped the new Boss of Everything and Everybody (as he soon became known) to precisely the degree that a fly stops a locomotive. Van Horne quickly spotted graft among several important employees. They drew their time. Then he opened up on his engineering staff. He fired Thomas Lafayette Rosser, the Confederate general who was his chief engineer, and then calmly took on that job himself. When his chief location engineer, J. H. E. Secretan, reasonably pointed out that Van Horne's lack of precise engineering knowledge might not be in the best interests of the company, the boss went off like a track torpedo. "Engineers," he roared, "bah! You get so all-fired tied up with log-tables that you can't talk a plain man's lingo. God knows the Canadians are bad enough but by the Lord Harry, Secretan, you English engineers take the cake! Hell's bones, man, if I could teach a sectionman to run a transit, I wouldn't have a single damned engineer around the place!"

And yet, somehow, this and similar rudenesses begat an inexplicable loyalty to this "damned, Yankee alien." One by one, his men began to realize that Van Horne was the most versatile man any of them had ever encountered.

Van Horne's life ran in at least six directions at once. The miracle was that he never seemed

confused. He was a master railroader of such ability that even his worst enemies acknowledged his superiority. At fourteen, he was so expert at telegraphy that when Lincoln came to his home town, Van Horne was chosen to put the president's Abolition speech on the wire. This skill he never lost, and often he would take a message directly from the sounder and have his reply written out before the astonished operator had written out the original. Rocks and fossils fascinated him and his knowledge was detailed enough to gain the respect of two famous geologists, Louis Agassiz, of Harvard, and James Geikie, of Edinburgh. He was a wicked satirical cartoonist who never spared his friends. He drew himself as an elephant, despite his uncanny resemblance to Edward VII. Of his oil painting, the artist Percy Woodcock was moved to say, "Van Horne painted as the birds sing, naturally and enjoyably." From this he went on to collect the oils of masters, and toward the end of his life his mansion on Sherbrooke Street in Montreal housed a fine collection indeed.

Between these major activities, Van Horne squeezed in long and elaborate practical jokes on his friends, card tricks and sleight-of-hand for his children and finally his grandchild. But his greatest minor skill was poker. He played against his staff all through the construction days and his greatest joy was to "clean out the boys." After an all-night session, when the boys were yawning and ready for sleep, the chief would tidy up and be ready, willing and more than able to face another sixteen-hour day. "Sleep," he would say, "is only a habit," or "Why go to bed? You miss a lot."

Forty-six amazing months did it. On a chill, wet seventh of November, 1885, in Eagle Pass at Craigellachie, the Last Spike was ready for the sledge. Taxed by some because there was no gold spike to drive and few official dignitaries to watch, Van Horne snorted, "Our last spike will be just as good an iron one as there is between Montreal and Vancouver. And anyone who wants to see it driven will have to pay full fare!" Donald A. Smith did the honours; Van Horne made the speech, a laconic gem. "All I can say is that the work has been well done in every way." Fifteen words; more, he would have considered a rank waste of the company's time.

From then on, many of the company's servants sat back, content with their new road. Not Van Horne. "Canada," he said with his customary drive, "is doing business on a back street! We must put her on a thoroughfare!" And he did. Between 1885 and the day of his retirement in 1910 he created traffic by building branch lines; encouraging immigrants; starting experimental farms for pioneer farmers ("Raise less hell and more wheat"); buying mines; building hotels ("We can't export our scenery so let's import our tourists"); building more boxcars for increased western wheat haulage ("The hopper is too big for the spout"); writing the company's first advertising ("HOW HIGH WE LIVE," *SAID THE DUKE TO THE PRINCE, ON THE CANADIAN PACIFIC RAILWAY*"); building trans-Atlantic and trans-Pacific steamships. And in 1900, when there seemed to be nothing more to accomplish, Van Horne took a holiday in Cuba and built another railroad there.

Born an American, he became a naturalized Canadian. And yet he was neither. From that freezing New Year's Eve of 1881, he was first, last and always a Canadian Pacific man. They had written an impossible contract; he had simply fulfilled it. "Go sell your boots and buy CPR stock," was his invariable advice. Small wonder there was a stir in Montreal when Sir William Van Horne, KCMG, died on September 11, 1915.

Representatives from many governments and the British royal family paid their respects. At an appointed hour all traffic on the gigantic system, which he had created, was braked to a five-minute stop in silent homage. The cortège was a moving spectacle as it left his home and wound its way slowly to his other home—the Canadian Pacific Railway Company's Windsor Street station.

And so he left on a special train and in his private car, *Saskatchewan*, with a clear track and a hookful of "31s" to prove it, running extra, just as it had always been. His final train order was a "terminal clearance" at Joliet, Illinois, where he had been born in 1843, and where they were to bury him.

# James Shaver Woodsworth

1874-1942

The conscience of Canada, he is generally credited with laying the foundation for the country's social welfare legislation, though he himself never held office. Born a minister's son in Etobicoke, near Toronto, he was ordained in the Methodist Church in 1896. He switched from the ministry to social welfare work after a few years and in 1919 became deeply involved in the Winnipeg General Strike. He was arrested and jailed for sedition – a charge that was later dropped. In 1921 he was elected Member of Parliament for Winnipeg North (later North Centre), a post he held until his death. He became leader of the Co-operative Commonwealth Federation, Canada's socialist party, in 1932.

# *The Saintly Rebel*

*by* M. J. COLDWELL

James Shaver Woodsworth was a great Canadian whose roots lay deep in the soil and history of our country. No private member of the House of Commons has ever exerted as profound an influence on Canada's social evolution as the dedicated man who for twenty-one years represented Winnipeg North Centre.

For the causes he espoused he worked unceasingly and, when necessary, was prepared to suffer and to stand alone. This he did on many occasions. We remember that September afternoon when the House of Commons approved of Canada's participation in the war against Hitler. When the fateful vote was called, Woodsworth rose and stood alone against it. So great was the respect the House had for him that no jeers greeted his unpopular and courageous decision. Less than an hour before, the prime minister had called him "an ornament to any democratic institution." For years he had declared that war settled nothing. Today one asks, "Was he so wrong?"

His speech opposing Canada's entry into the war was his last major effort in the House of Commons. A few months later the House was dissolved. Woodsworth was re-elected in the general election of March, 1940. His majority of a scant 125 votes was made possible by the support he received from men serving in the armed forces overseas. Nothing could have pleased him more. He felt the soldiers understood him and that he had received a vote of confidence from them. This thought helped him bear the effects of a crippling stroke which, for his two remaining years, denied him further participation in the work of parliament.

Radical though he was, he was proud of his United Empire Loyalist ancestry. On a visit to his Winnipeg home, I once expressed surprise to see an ancient broadsword hanging from the wall. He took it down and drew it from its scabbard to show the marks left by a grindstone when his grandfather prepared to fight William Lyon Mackenzie in 1837. Woodsworth himself would have sympathized with the rebel, Mackenzie. As he ran his fingers along the blade, he remarked that perhaps he should take it to Ottawa. It might be useful in dealing with Mackenzie's grandson, William Lyon Mackenzie King. But there was no need; Woodsworth's tongue could be sharper than his grandfather's sword, although he was invariably courteous in debate.

In his early manhood he had every opportunity to settle down in a comfortable pulpit. Instead, he chose to champion the underprivileged; to apply the teachings of Christ's social gospel. He was influenced in this by the friends he made when studying at Mansfield College, Oxford, and by his short stay at Mansfield House in the London slums. He had been brought into close contact with devoted men and women who were applying the social gospel, opposing the Boer War and promoting new political ideas that were later used by the Labour Party. His youth in his father's home had already enabled him to understand the difficulties and hardships that beset the early prairie pioneers.

Physically frail in appearance, he was indefatigable. In his active years as a parliamentarian, he travelled constantly to meet the people he served and loved. His journeys by train were made in day coaches. By night, he would take a tourist sleeper – most frequently an upper berth. Mrs. Woodsworth, or sometimes friends he visited along the way, would provide him with a bag of sandwiches and he would make himself a cup of tea in the kitchen provided for those who could not afford the dining car. This was not because he was parsimonious. Indeed, he often paid his own travelling expenses, and made donations he could ill afford to labour and socialist organizations. Later, when he was in failing health, the CCF national office provided him with tickets for first-class sleeper accommodation. He cancelled the reservations and returned the tickets, requesting that the proceeds be used for party purposes.

In the autumn of 1939 I travelled with him from Winnipeg to Fort William. He was not well and was obviously very tired. He tried to rest curled up on a coach seat. I asked the conductor if there was a chair car on the train. He referred me to the buffet car – chairs were available there. I returned and suggested to Mr. Woodsworth that he take a chair. He said he preferred to remain like others in the day coach. He often travelled alone with a couple of suitcases mainly filled with literature for distribution at his meetings. Heavy as they were, he carried them himself.

In parliament he was faithful in attendance, seizing every opportunity to raise his voice against injustice or to advance policies he believed were in the interests of the underprivileged or of Canada. The Indians, the Orientals of the Pacific Coast, the Doukhobors and all who suffered discrimination had in Woodsworth a powerful friend. In 1937 anti-Oriental propaganda was at its height. At Victoria, in the by-election of November, 1937, Mr. Woodsworth spoke in support of the CCF candidate, King Gordon. He made a powerful plea for the removal of the electoral disabilities suffered by citizens of Oriental origin or descent in British Columbia, and demanded the repeal of the discriminatory clauses against them in the Immigration Act. This was the right but unpopular position to take. As he stood, a frail but defiant figure with arm and pointed beard outstretched, our candidate whispered in my ear, "Doesn't he remind you of the prophet Amos?" We were proud of him. We lost the by-election by ninety votes.

He was a firm and fearless defender of human rights and fundamental freedoms for all. He went to parliament determined to rid the Statute Books of Section 98 and the amendment to the Immigration Act, both of which had been passed in 1919 by a panic-stricken government demoralized by the Winnipeg General Strike. It was not until 1936 that, after the House of Commons had three times agreed to the repeal of Section 98, the Senate gave its approval also.

The achievements of J. S. Woodsworth in the public life of Canada, his work in laying the foundations of the social-welfare state, are part of the history of our country. They reveal, too, the strength of his character and his devotion to the cause of human betterment and progress. He was a man many of us remember with gratitude, pride, and reverence.

A NOTE ON THE AUTHORS

A NOTE ON THE ARTIST

# THE AUTHORS

*In this book, whenever possible, the editors have tried to choose authors who have had some connection with their subject matter. In a few instances, however, the authors have been chosen simply because they write well.*

ROBERT THOMAS ALLEN (*Alexander Graham Bell*), whose humorous articles and books have a broad readership in both Canada and the United States, is a restless Canadian who spends his time in Toronto, in Florida, in Omemee, in California and on the telephone.

LEONARD BERTIN (*Sir Frederick Banting*), one of the continent's most respected science and medical writers, has travelled in thirty-five countries and on five continents in the course of his research. He is, at present, on the staff of the University of Toronto.

PIERRE BERTON (*Joseph Burr Tyrrell*) has travelled over much of the country that his subject traversed–but rarely on foot. Northern-born, he holds two Governor-General's Awards for creative non-fiction about the north, and is editor-in-chief of the Canadian Centennial Library.

HARRY BRUCE (*Sir Sandford Fleming*) the son of a distinguished Canadian journalist and poet, has worked variously for the Ottawa *Journal*, the *Globe and Mail*, *Maclean's* and *Saturday Night*. He is now managing editor of *The Canadian*.

JUNE CALLWOOD (*Sir Charles Saunders*) is Canada's best-known woman journalist. Besides several hundred articles for Canadian and U.S. periodicals, she has to her credit four children, a husband, and an unemotional study of the human emotions.

M. J. COLDWELL (*J. S. Woodsworth*) succeeded as national leader of their party the man about whom he writes with such affection. A teacher by profession and a politician by inclination, he is now a member of the Queen's Privy Council for Canada.

JAMES COLEMAN (*Lord Strathcona*) was raised in the bosom of the Canadian Pacific Railway. His father was the fifth chairman and president of the company. One of Canada's best-known sportswriters and broadcasters, Mr. Coleman is at present Toronto-based columnist for the Southam Newspapers.

DONALD CREIGHTON (*Harold Innis*) succeeds his subject as Canada's most distinguished living historian–and certainly her most honoured. His many awards include the fifteen-thousand-dollar Molson Prize. A former head of the history department of the University of Toronto, he is renowned for his two-volume biography of Sir John A. Macdonald.

ROBERTSON DAVIES (*George Grant*) is a man of parts–novelist, playwright, lecturer, editor and critic. He began his career as an actor with the Old Vic in London and matured as editor of the Peterborough *Examiner*. He is at present Master of Massey College at the University of Toronto.

MARCEL DUBE (*Alain Grandbois*) is one of French Canada's best-known playwrights and bon vivants. A former editor of *Perspectives*, he now devotes all his working hours to theatre and television. He has produced several dozen plays, many of them award-winners.

PETER GZOWSKI (*Cardinal Léger*) was Quebec editor of *Maclean's* when he first interviewed the Cardinal and began the series of reports that introduced the phrase "quiet revolution" to the national press. His forebear, the railway- and bridge-builder Sir Casimir Gzowski, was a candidate for inclusion among the subjects of this book.

ARTHUR HAILEY (*Timothy Eaton*) is a best-selling novelist and television playwright who has long been fascinated by large institutions. Having investigated a big hospital and a big hotel, he is now investigating a big airport. Next on his list, he says, is a big department store.

WILLIAM KILBOURN (*Emily Carr*) is a Canadian historian whose books include the award-winning biography of William Lyon Mackenzie, *The Firebrand*, and *The Making of the Nation* in this series. Chairman of the department of humanities at York University, he makes a hobby and occasionally a profession of collecting and reviewing Canadian painting.

MAURICE LEBEL (*Sir Thomas Chapais*), past president of the Royal Society of Canada, is a member of our selection committee whose credentials are chronicled more fully earlier in this volume.

KEN LEFOLII (*Gratien Gélinas*) studied French Canada first-hand as a resident correspondent in Quebec. A former managing editor of *Liberty* and editor-in-chief of *Maclean's*, he is now managing editor of the Canadian Centennial Library.

ROGER LEMELIN (*Joseph E. Bernier*) is perhaps the best-known writer in French Canada. His novel *The Town Below* brought him critical acclaim and his long-running radio and television series, *The Plouffe Family*, made his name a household word. He was once champion junior tumbler of Canada.

GRANT MCCONACHIE (*Clennell H. "Punch" Dickins*), the late president of Canadian Pacific Airlines, began his career as a Yukon bush pilot. His pioneer work made the wartime Northwest Staging Route possible and his executive ability produced CPA. Like the subject of his article, he held a McKee Trophy for "long and outstanding service in the field of Canadian aviation."

BRIAN MOORE (*Gabrielle Roy*) is the Belfast-born author of several novels, all of which have gained critical acclaim. Though he now lives in the United States he is generally claimed (by Canadians) as a Canadian author, partly because he once worked in Montreal and partly because he won the Governor-General's Award for fiction with *The Luck of Ginger Coffey*, for which he also wrote the screenplay.

ERIC NICOL (*Stephen Butler Leacock*) is that rare bird, an authentic Canadian humorist – and he has three Leacock Medals for humour to prove it. A syndicated columnist for the Vancouver *Province*, he has produced eleven books, all of them best-sellers.

DR. WILDER GRAVES PENFIELD (*Sir William Osler*) is Canada's most distinguished medical scientist and one of the world's leading brain surgeons. He was director of the famous Montreal Neurological Institute between 1934 and 1960. In his spare time he writes historical novels.

JAMES REANEY (*E. J. "Ned" Pratt*), a leading Canadian poet, is three times winner of the Governor-General's Award. He is at present on the staff of Middlesex College, University of Western Ontario, London.

CLAUDE RYAN (*Henri Bourassa*) is a social scientist turned editor. He is a graduate of the University of Montreal's school of social science, a student of church history (Georgian University, Rome) and has been with Henri Bourassa's paper, *Le Devoir*, since 1962. He was appointed publisher in 1964.

HAROLD TOWN (*Tom Thomson*) is both the *enfant terrible* of Canadian painting and a member of the establishment. A member of the Royal Canadian Academy and a perennial winner of international awards, he contributes essays and prefaces to books and periodicals, and appears frequently on television. He is the author of *Enigmas*.

TOMMY TWEED (*Sir William Cornelius Van Horne*) is a film and radio writer, actor and historian who has been actively engaged in broadcasting since 1935. A fellow of the rarely publicized Canadian Footnote Society, he is well known, among other things, for his radio and television biographies of Van Horne, "The Brass Pounder from Illinois."

MAJ.-GEN. F. F. WORTHINGTON (*Sir Arthur Currie*) is one of Canada's most colourful soldiers. He sailed before the mast at the turn of the century and fought Pancho Villa in Mexico. An early advocate of the tank, he organized and trained the Canadian Fourth Armoured Division during World War II.

## THE ARTIST

⋘

**FRANKLIN ARBUCKLE, PRCA, OSA** is Canada's best-known illustrator. He has travelled in every corner of the country on assignments for Canadian periodicals and corporations. His magazine covers are well known and his paintings have been seen in most major Canadian shows. His murals for the Canadian Pacific Railway, the Steel Company of Canada and the city hall of Hamilton, Ontario, have attracted wide attention as have his tapestries for the Ontario head office of the Royal Bank of Canada in Toronto. A departmental director of the Ontario College of Art, he has twice been awarded the Jessie Dow prize of the Montreal Museum of Fine Arts. He also holds four major art club awards and the International Business Machines medal.

## PICTURE CREDITS

Order of appearance in the text of pictures listed here is left to right, top to bottom. After the first recording, principal sources are credited under these abbreviations: John De Visser, JDV; The Globe & Mail, GM; Ontario Archives, OA; Henri Paul, HP; Public Archives of Canada, PA; Toronto Star Syndicate, TS.

Cover, Franklin Arbuckle / p. 6, John De Visser / p. 8, Ralph Greenhill Collection (from Miller Services); Ontario Archives; Public Archives / p. 9, PA; Toronto Public Libraries; Bill & Jean Newton / p. 13, Toronto Star Syndicate; Bridgens Photographers, Winnipeg Free Press; National Film Board; TS; Ontario Hydro; TS; Wide World-Wheeler Services; Alberta Government Photograph from the Ernest Brown Collection; TS / p. 14, JDV / p. 16, JDV / p. 17, JDV / p. 18, JDV / p. 19, JDV / p. 23, PA; Department of Information, University of Toronto / p. 27, The Bell Telephone Co. of Canada (Telephone Historical Collection) / p. 31, PA / p. 35, Henri Paul / p. 39, British Columbia Provincial Archives / p. 43, Maurice Lebel / p. 47, PA / p. 51, National Aviation Museum, Ottawa / p. 55, Archives, Eaton's of Canada / p. 59, PA / p. 63, Comédie Canadienne Inc.; HP / p. 67, Alain Grandbois / p. 71, Douglas Library Archives, Queen's University / p. 75, Mrs. Harold Innis, Innis College / p. 79, Karsh, Ottawa (from Miller Services) / p. 83, S. Appetiti, Rome / p. 87, Johns Hopkins University / p. 91, The Globe & Mail, Toronto / p. 95, Beauchemin Publishers; Basil Zarov / p. 99, PA / p. 103, PA / p. 107, John Boyd / p. 111, GM / p. 115, Thomas Harkness & Sons, Rolph-Clark-Stone Limited / p. 119, Karsh, Ottawa.

Excerpts from COLLECTED POEMS OF E. J. PRATT by permission of The Estate of E. J. Pratt and The Macmillan Company of Canada Limited.

## NOTE ON EMILY CARR

This article is largely based on an unpublished essay about Emily Carr by Rosemary Kilbourn, a painter and engraver. The author is grateful to Clarke, Irwin and Co. for permission to use the two short quotations from the works of Emily Carr.

Type for the text of this book is 11 point Pilgrim,
composed by T. H. Best Printing Company Limited.
It was printed in Canada on Cartier Litho paper
by Litho-Print Limited.
The case was printed by Sampson Matthews Limited,
and bound by T. H. Best Limited